Beyond the Shiny Object

Journey to Healing for Male Survivors

Jeffrey Shearer, PhD

Acknowledgements

First and foremost, I want to express my deepest gratitude to the many male survivors I have had the privilege of supporting over the years. Your courage, resilience, and willingness to share your journeys have profoundly inspired and taught me. This book would not exist without you, and I am forever honored to have walked alongside you in your healing.

I also want to acknowledge the incredible professionals who have supported and guided me throughout my journey. Your insight, encouragement, and collaboration have been invaluable. A special thank you to Elly, the chairperson of my dissertation committee, whose guidance and support were instrumental in shaping the research that forms the foundation of this book. I am deeply grateful for your belief in this work and your encouragement along the way.

A heartfelt thank you to Joni and Robin for your dedication and care in editing this book—your expertise has truly brought my vision to life.

Most importantly, I want to thank my family, whose unwavering love and belief in me have been my anchor. To my two amazing sons, Ian and Aidan, your light and love fuel my every endeavor. And to my wonderful husband, Rudy, your steadfast support and partnership mean the world to me. Together, you are my greatest source of strength and inspiration.

This book is for all of you.

Disclaimer

The stories shared in this book are inspired by the experiences of real men who have faced and overcome significant struggles. To protect their privacy, names, identifying details, and certain aspects of their stories have been changed or combined. These adaptations are intended to illustrate key concepts and provide deeper understanding, while honoring the courage and resilience of the men who shared their journeys.

Preface

For over three decades, my career has been dedicated to serving vulnerable populations, with a deep focus on male survivors of sexual abuse and interpersonal trauma. My journey began with the founding of Tykes & Teens, a nonprofit organization committed to providing high-quality mental health services to children and families, especially those overlooked by systems like foster care and juvenile justice. Throughout this work, my personal mission remained focused on understanding and supporting the healing of male trauma survivors.

Through my work with adolescents in foster care, I witnessed how trauma distorted their ability to form healthy relationships and undermined their sense of self-worth. Later, in working with adult male survivors, I saw how trauma affected their sexual development and intimate connections. These experiences reinforced the need for tools to help survivors rebuild their understanding of healthy relationships. *Beyond the Shiny Object* is the culmination of this journey, offering a framework for therapists and counselors to address trauma's deeper impact, using concepts from family systems theory, trauma research, and healthy sexual development.

After three decades of experience working with male survivors, I pursued a PhD focused on sexual and interpersonal trauma in men. This work helped me integrate developmental, relational, and sexual dynamics into a cohesive model for healing. This book is inspired by the resilience of survivors and is a call to move beyond superficial solutions toward deeper healing. It is my hope that it will equip professionals with practical tools and raise awareness of the profound effects of trauma on male survivors.

CONTENTS

John's Story

John sat across from me in my office, a man in his early 50s with a posture that seemed to carry the weight of his years. His eyes, weary and distant, hinted at the turmoil beneath the surface. He was here because his wife, Carole, had discovered—again—that he had been paying for prostitutes. This was the second time in their 25-year marriage that he had been caught, and now the burden of that discovery hung heavily. Carole had made it clear that if John wanted to stay married, he needed to participate in treatment. But as I observed him in those first sessions, it was evident that he wasn't convinced he had a problem. His resistance and hesitation were palpable.

Carole, through her own therapy, had come to believe that John was a sex addict. She was desperate for him to seek help, and for the past three months, John had been seeing a therapist who specialized in sex addiction. However, those sessions had only deepened his feelings of shame. He described how the addiction model wasn't resonating with him; it felt as though it was stripping him down to his worst parts without offering any real path to rebuild. He understood why Carole felt the way she did—he had betrayed her trust, and she was right to demand transparency. He had given her access to all his online activities, but instead of feeling like a step toward healing, it made him feel trapped, as if he were a prisoner in his own life.

Despite everything, John loved Carole deeply. He wanted their relationship to work, not just for his sake but for their children's too. But he was struggling to reconcile the man he wanted to be with the man who kept making these destructive choices. There was something deeper at play, something that the label of "sex addict" didn't seem to touch.

As we continued our sessions, there was a moment when John finally opened up about his childhood. He revealed that he had been sexually abused by his stepfather when he was a boy. The way he spoke, the hesitation, the pain in his voice—it was clear that this trauma was a wound he had never truly addressed. He admitted that he thought the abuse might be related to the behaviors he was now being labeled an addict for, but the connection felt murky and confusing to him.

Together, we began to explore the function of his behavior—not from the perspective of addiction, but from a place of curiosity and compassion. I asked him what he was trying to achieve through these actions. How were they serving him? As we unpacked these questions, John repeated some of the ideas he had learned in addiction therapy, but there was a clear disconnect. He could recite the patterns and cycles, but I could see that he didn't truly believe in them—not in a way that would lead to genuine change.

This was a pivotal moment in our work together. The focus shifted from trying to fit John into a predefined model to understanding him as a whole person, with a unique history and a complex set of needs. We began to look at the shiny objects in John's life—the things that drew his attention and pulled him away from his pain. These weren't just distractions; they were coping mechanisms, ways of avoiding deeper wounds that had been festering for decades.

As John began to see his behaviors in this new light, a path to healing started to emerge—not as a battle against an addiction, but as a journey toward understanding and integrating the parts of himself that he had long ignored. The road ahead was still uncertain, but for the first time in a long while, John felt like he was beginning to understand the real problem, and with that, the possibility of a real solution.

"Beyond the Shiny Object" is about these journeys—about moving past the labels and the shame to explore the deeper reasons behind our behaviors, and finding a path to genuine healing. For John, and for so many others, this exploration is the key to reclaiming their lives and their relationships. As a therapist, my role is to create the space where this exploration can happen, to guide my clients as they navigate the complexities of their pasts, and to help them find their way to a more integrated and whole sense of self.

Section 1:

THE INTERPLAY OF TRAUMA, ATTACHMENT, AND GENDER: A FRAMEWORK FOR HEALING RELATIONSHIPS

Chapter 1

THE SHINY OBJECT PHENOMENON: DISTRACTION FROM DEEPER HEALING

We must understand the concepts of the mind. The human mind is an extraordinary instrument, shaped by layers of complexity over time, to function with remarkable efficiency. It constantly seeks the easiest and most effective ways to process information, allowing us to react quickly to our surroundings, ensuring our safety, and propelling us forward in life. However, this remarkable efficiency also comes with its own set of challenges. In our quest for survival, our minds often focus on the most immediate and attention-grabbing elements in our environment—what we might call the "shiny objects." These distractions can sometimes lead us away from deeper truths about ourselves and the world around us.

The essence of the "shiny object" concept lies in its ability to divert attention from the core issue at hand. In the context of interpersonal trauma in men, the "shiny object" represents the surface-level manifestations—such as elevated suicide rates, substance abuse, and other destructive behaviors that distract us from addressing the deeper, underlying problem: trauma, and more specifically, interpersonal trauma.

When we explore how trauma impacts men, we see a clear connection between trauma and the prevalence of depression, suicide, and substance use. These issues often intersect, creating a vicious cycle of self-destruction. However, societal focus tends to zero in on the alarming statistics—like the fact that men are four times more likely to die by suicide—or on the need to treat substance abuse through abstinence programs. While these are critical issues, they are the "shiny objects" that draw attention away from the root cause, which is often deeply embedded trauma.

Interpersonal trauma, particularly when it is unrecognized or untreated, is often the driving force behind many surface-level issues, including addiction and suicidal behavior. Yet, it frequently remains in the background, overshadowed by more visible symptoms. In many cases, the focus of treatment becomes centered on managing these symptoms—emphasizing sobriety for addiction or addressing depression through medication to reduce suicide risk. While these approaches are vital, they often neglect the essential work of addressing the underlying trauma itself.

This oversight allows the trauma to persist, perpetuating the very behaviors and outcomes we aim to prevent. By focusing solely on the symptoms, such as achieving sobriety or lowering suicide rates, without delving into the root cause—interpersonal trauma—the core issue remains unaddressed. For men, this is particularly insidious. Societal expectations often discourage emotional vulnerability, leading to trauma being left untreated or unrecognized. The result is a cycle where the trauma continues to drive the destructive behaviors and mental health challenges that surface later in life.

To truly break this cycle, it is crucial to shift the focus of treatment from merely managing symptoms to also confronting and healing the trauma that lies beneath. Without this deeper work, the interventions may only provide temporary relief, leaving the underlying trauma to manifest in new, potentially more harmful ways.

In essence, the "shiny object" distracts us from the profound and complex impact of interpersonal trauma, steering the conversation toward symptoms rather than causes. To truly help men who are suffering, it is crucial to shift the focus away from these distractions and toward the underlying trauma that fuels these destructive behaviors.

Renowned physician and author Gabor Maté has extensively explored the intricacies of human needs, particularly focusing on two fundamental drives: the need for a sense of belonging and the drive to be authentic. Maté suggests that when these two core needs—belonging and authenticity—come into conflict, it creates profound distress within the individual. This internal conflict can manifest in various ways, often leading us to seek solace in superficial distractions, the proverbial shiny objects, rather than addressing the underlying issues that cause our distress.

This book, *Beyond the Shiny Object*, seeks to explore how we, as individuals, develop our sense of self. It delves into both biological and experiential factors that shape who we are, examining the constant interplay between nature and nurture. Throughout the history of psychology, there has been a persistent debate over whether we are primarily products of our biology or our experiences. This dichotomy, often framed as "nature versus nurture," suggests that we must think in binary terms, which is a simplification our minds prefer due to their efficiency. However, it is increasingly clear that the reality is far more nuanced, residing somewhere in the grey area between these two extremes.

In this book, we will explore the macro-level influences on our understanding of self, focusing on how our culture shapes our identity and behaviors. Culture operates on multiple levels, from the immediate microcosm of our families and social circles to the broader systems in which we are embedded, such as schools, workplaces, religious institutions, and social clubs. These systems exert powerful influences on our sense of belonging and authenticity. Moreover, in today's interconnected world, global factors such as social media, politics, and nationalism also play significant roles in shaping our identities and the conflicts we experience within them.

While the broader themes of belonging, authenticity, and cultural influences are crucial in understanding human behavior, *Beyond the Shiny Object* takes a specific and deeply necessary focus on the understudied area of interpersonal sexual trauma in males. This dynamic, shaped by the very variables discussed above, warrants a deeper exploration due to its profound implications on the mental health and well-being of men, particularly in the context of societal gender norms and the integration of trauma.

Interpersonal sexual trauma is a woefully understudied issue, especially when it comes to male victims. The lack of research and understanding is not only a gap in the literature but a reflection of deeper societal attitudes toward gender and trauma. Cultural norms around masculinity often dictate that men should be strong, stoic, and invulnerable. These expectations can create an environment where men feel unable to acknowledge, let alone address, the trauma they have experienced. This is particularly true when the trauma is of a sexual nature, which conflicts sharply with traditional gender norms.

The impact of these gender norms on how men integrate trauma cannot be overstated. In many cultures, there is an unspoken expectation that men must handle their problems on their own, without seeking help. This stoic ideal, while admired in many contexts, and often reframed as resilience, becomes deeply problematic when applied to the experience of trauma. It leads to isolation, shame, and a reluctance to seek the necessary support. When the trauma involves sexual trauma, the stigma is even more intense. The very idea of a man being a victim of interpersonal sexual trauma challenges entrenched notions of masculinity, making it even more difficult for men to process and heal from their experiences.

The struggle of men to find a space where they can recover and explore what it means to be victimized is currently being explored at a deeper level as we navigate the epidemic crisis of suicide among our military veterans. Military culture, with its emphasis on strength, resilience, and self-reliance, mirrors broader societal expectations of masculinity. The trauma experienced by many veterans fits into the gendered norm of being victimized by war and violence. However, even within this context, there is a significant gap in recognizing the need for men to have a space to recover and explore their trauma, particularly when it involves interpersonal sexual trauma.

Research indicates that veterans with a history of interpersonal trauma—meaning they were harmed within the context of a relationship—are at a significantly higher risk of being diagnosed with Post-Traumatic Stress Disorder (PTSD) and may struggle to perform their duties to their full capabilities in the military. This suggests that military trauma tends to exacerbate pre-existing issues rather than create them. In contrast, those who experience military trauma alone, without a prior history of interpersonal trauma, tend to recover more quickly and with less intervention.

The distinct difference lies in the nature of the trauma: interpersonal trauma, which involves betrayal and harm from someone within a trusted relationship, has a much deeper psychological impact compared to life-threatening situations encountered in combat, which typically involve an unknown enemy. The personal and relational betrayal inherent in interpersonal trauma can shatter one's sense of trust and safety, making recovery more complex and prolonged. On the other hand, trauma from combat with an unknown entity, while severe, does not usually involve this profound breach of trust, allowing for a comparatively quicker recovery process. This highlights the unique and devastating effects of interpersonal trauma on mental health, particularly in the context of military service.

One can only imagine the compounded difficulty when we add the layer of interpersonal trauma through the lens of sexual trauma. Interpersonal trauma, by its nature, occurs within the context of relationships. It involves a betrayal of trust and a violation of boundaries that can have a profound impact on an individual's ability to form and maintain healthy relationships in the future. Healing from interpersonal trauma, therefore, often requires engaging in new, healthy relationships that can provide a corrective emotional experience. However, because the injury occurred within the context of a relationship, and because the concept of authenticity can be weaponized by offenders to manipulate their victims, it is understandable that many survivors may avoid deep, intimate relationships altogether. This avoidance can make it nearly impossible to achieve the kind of relational healing that is necessary for recovery.

In this book, we will explore these issues on multiple levels. At the macro level, we will examine how societal gender norms and cultural expectations influence the way men experience and integrate trauma. We will also look at the role of institutions—such as the military, religious organizations, and mental health services—in either supporting or hindering the recovery process. For example, military culture often prioritizes resilience and self-sufficiency, which can make it difficult for veterans to acknowledge and seek help for trauma, especially when that trauma is of a sexual nature. Similarly, many religious organizations may emphasize forgiveness and reconciliation, which can be problematic as it can be seen as a toxic positive response and avoidance when dealing with the profound betrayal involved in sexual trauma.

At the micro level, we will delve into the personal experiences of male survivors of sexual trauma, exploring how their identities have been shaped by both their biology and their experiences. This includes an examination of how attachment theory and personality traits influence their ability to form relationships, as well as how trauma can impact the structure and function of the brain. We will also consider the role of authenticity in the healing process, recognizing that while authenticity is often seen as a key component of psychological health, it can be a double-edged sword for trauma survivors. Offenders often use a facade of authenticity to manipulate and control their victims, making it difficult for survivors to trust their own instincts or to engage authentically with others.

A crucial aspect of this exploration is understanding how the concepts of belonging and authenticity intersect with the experience of trauma. For many male survivors, trauma disrupts their sense of belonging, as they harbor a secret that makes them feel fundamentally different and defective, unworthy of inclusion. The cultural narrative that men should be strong and invulnerable intensifies this sense of defectiveness, leading to isolation and shame, as survivors feel they have failed to meet societal expectations. This isolation is further compounded by the nature of sexual trauma, which often involves profound betrayal and a loss of trust in others.

Healing from this kind of trauma requires more than just individual therapy or support. It requires a cultural shift in the way we understand and respond to male survivors of interpersonal sexual trauma. This includes challenging the societal norms that perpetuate silence and shame, creating spaces where men can feel safe from judgement to share their experiences and seek support, and providing education and training for professionals who work with trauma survivors. It also means recognizing that healing is not a linear process, but a journey that requires time, patience, and the support of a compassionate community.

In *Beyond the Shiny Object*, we will also explore the role of relationships in the healing process. While trauma often disrupts relationships, it is through relationships that healing can occur. This book will examine how survivors can rebuild trust, both in themselves and in others, and how they can learn to engage authentically in relationships after experiencing such profound betrayal. We will look at the role of therapy in this process, as well as the importance of peer support and community involvement.

Ultimately, *Beyond the Shiny Object* is a call to move beyond the superficial distractions that often capture our attention and to engage with the deeper, more challenging issues that shape our identities and our lives. By exploring the complex interplay between biology, experience, culture, and trauma, this book aims to provide a deeper understanding of the human mind and the process of healing. It is an invitation to look beyond the shiny objects that so often distract us and to engage with the real work of understanding ourselves and supporting each other on the journey to recovery.

Chapter 2

THE HIDDEN STRUGGLES OF MALE SURVIVORS: UNPACKING TRAUMA, ATTACHMENT, AND MASCULINITY

Interpersonal sexual trauma in males is a deeply complex and often misunderstood issue that intersects with societal norms, gender expectations, and the intricacies of the victim-offender relationship. Despite the prevalence of such trauma, many male victims face significant barriers to being believed or are wrongly judged as participants in their own abuse. This issue is further complicated by the fact that, particularly for children, 90% of victims know their offenders well and often return to them multiple times. This dynamic reveals that the trauma itself is not merely an act of violence but can also involve a distorted form of connection, where victims may receive something from the experience—such as a sense of belonging or perceived love—that contrasts sharply with the offender's motivations. The public, however, often fails to grasp this complexity, leading to the imposition of harmful gender-specific narratives on the abuse.

When the offender is female, society may mistakenly view the abuse as a rite of passage or an accomplishment, reinforcing toxic masculinity and downplaying the victim's trauma. Conversely, when the offender is male, society grapples with how to respond appropriately. On one hand, there is a tendency to demonize the offender, which can create conflicting emotions in the victim. The victim may recognize that the offender's actions are wrong, yet simultaneously feel a strong connection and a desire to protect them. This internal conflict is further complicated if the abusive behavior felt pleasurable, leading the child to question themselves and wonder if something is inherently wrong with them. These complex emotions often drive the victim to keep the abuse a secret, believing they are somehow complicit in the situation.

Adding to this confusion is the societal narrative that male offenders are often former victims themselves. A child who is aware of this may fear being labeled an offender in the future, as they too have been victimized. When the abuse involves a same-sex offender, it can also lead to confusion about the child's own sexuality, intensifying the urge to keep the abuse hidden. These gendered narratives not only reinforce harmful stereotypes but also contribute to the underreporting of male sexual abuse, leaving many victims without the necessary support and validation.

Understanding the prevalence of childhood sexual abuse among males poses a significant challenge due to varying data across different sources. Finkelhor's updated study in 2024 highlighted international rates ranging from 0% in some countries to as high as 29% in South Africa, illustrating the wide variability in reported prevalence rates. Despite these differences, Pereda's 2009 meta-analysis offers a more consistent estimate, suggesting that between 6.2% to 10.8% of males globally experience childhood sexual abuse. Dube's 2005 study, based on data from the Adverse Childhood Experiences (ACE) study, further underscores the gravity of the issue, reporting a male victimization rate of 16%. These statistics reflect the significant yet often hidden impact of sexual trauma on male survivors and highlight the need for a deeper understanding of the factors that contribute to their reluctance to report abuse.

A critical aspect of this reluctance is the underutilization of mental health services by men, which is exacerbated by societal pressures to conform to traditional masculine norms. According to the National Institute of Mental Health, one in five adults in the United States experiences a mental illness each year. While this affects both men and women, the prevalence of reported mental illness is lower in men (18.1%) compared to women (27.2%). However, these statistics mask a significant concern: men are far less likely to seek mental health treatment, and their issues often go untreated. This underutilization of services leads to severe repercussions, including higher rates of depression, suicide, and substance abuse among men. In 2020, Mental Health America reports that six million men in the U.S. are affected by depression annually, and men are four times more likely than women to die by suicide, with 79% of the 38,364 suicides in the U.S. being men.

These alarming statistics underline the importance of understanding the barriers that prevent men from seeking help. Traditional gender norms, which promote self-reliance, emotional stoicism, and strength, play a significant role in these barriers. These cultural pressures can lead male survivors of sexual trauma to avoid forming friendships or seeking treatment out of fear of being perceived as weak or unmasculine. This avoidance is often rooted in a coping mechanism designed to protect themselves from further harm or judgment.

Gender theory offers valuable insights into how these societal expectations shape the experiences of male survivors. Within the context of sexual trauma, traditional gender norms can exacerbate the challenges faced by male survivors, making it difficult for them to seek help or establish meaningful connections. This cultural pressure to conform to masculine ideals not only hinders their ability to heal but also perpetuates feelings of shame and isolation.

Trauma theory further elucidates the psychological and emotional impact of sexual trauma on individuals. For male survivors, the avoidance of intimate and authentic friendships can be a direct response to their traumatic experiences. Sexual trauma often leads to profound feelings of shame, guilt, and distrust, which can make it challenging for survivors to establish new connections. The fear of potential re-traumatization or betrayal may drive them to isolate themselves, avoiding the vulnerability that comes with forming close friendships. This isolation, while a protective measure, can also prevent them from accessing the support and care they need to heal.

The believability of male survivors' trauma narratives presents a significant challenge, one that is deeply intertwined with societal views on gender. Many men struggle with the credibility of their trauma stories, largely due to ingrained societal norms that cast doubt on their experiences. This skepticism is pervasive, extending beyond the general public and into the mental health system itself. Therapists, often influenced by these same societal norms, may unconsciously reinforce these biases, further complicating the path to validation and support for male survivors. This dynamic makes it even more challenging for men to receive the acknowledgment and help they desperately need.

Attachment theory provides another layer of understanding by examining how early attachment experiences shape individuals' patterns of relating to others. Male survivors of sexual trauma may have experienced disruptions in their attachment bonds, which can significantly impact their willingness to seek treatment. Attachment insecurity, characterized by a fear of rejection or abandonment, may lead survivors to avoid therapy or counseling due to concerns about judgment or re-traumatization. The fear of opening up and trusting others, deeply rooted in their attachment experiences, can further hinder their ability to seek the support they need.

One of the primary needs of human beings is to feel connected and to belong. For male survivors, the cost of maintaining a connection with an offender often comes at the expense of enduring interpersonal trauma. This painful trade-off underscores the complexity of the "shiny object" phenomenon, where the perceived benefits of connection and belonging are overshadowed by the profound harm caused by the abuse. To address this, it is essential to create a therapeutic environment that acknowledges and validates the unique experiences of male survivors.

The concept of countertransference, first introduced by Sigmund Freud, is particularly relevant in the treatment of male sexual abuse survivors. Countertransference refers to the therapist's emotional reactions to a client's trauma, which can significantly impact the treatment process. Therapists must be aware of their biases, triggers, and the societal influences that shape their perceptions of male survivors. By engaging in ongoing self-reflection, supervision, and education, therapists can ensure that their personal reactions do not interfere with providing empathetic, trauma-informed care. This approach is crucial in creating a safe therapeutic space where the client's experiences and needs remain at the forefront of treatment.

In conclusion, understanding the impact of interpersonal sexual trauma on males requires an integrated approach that considers gender theory, trauma theory, and attachment theory. Traditional gender norms, trauma responses, and attachment patterns all interact to shape the experiences of male survivors, influencing their ability to form friendships, seek treatment, and heal. By challenging societal expectations and addressing the unique challenges faced by male survivors, mental health professionals can create supportive environments that promote recovery and well-being. Moreover, by recognizing the potential for countertransference, therapists can provide care that is both empathetic and effective, helping male survivors navigate their complex trauma narratives and move toward healing.

In *Beyond the Shiny Object*, I explore the micro-level experiences of male survivors and examine the experiences of those in relationships with them, all within the broader context of societal norms and relational dynamics. Through this exploration, I have identified 15 key characteristics, which will be explored in section 2, that are vital for fostering healing in relationships with male survivors. These characteristics will be examined in-depth throughout the book, offering a framework for understanding and supporting male survivors. By delving into these aspects, *Beyond the Shiny Object* provides insights and guidance on navigating the complexities of healing and connection in relationships with male survivors.

Chapter 3:

ILLUMINATING THE PATH: THEORETICAL FOUNDATIONS FOR HEALING MALE SURVIVORS OF SEXUAL ABUSE

To deepen our understanding of the framework for treating male survivors of sexual abuse, we must delve into the profound impact of relationships on both the harm caused by interpersonal trauma and the potential for healing. By exploring various theoretical models—particularly trauma theory, gender theory, and attachment theory, and understanding sexual development—we can uncover the nuanced dynamics of human connections, which are central to both the wounds inflicted by trauma and the pathways to recovery. In doing so, we unlock the "shiny objects" within these concepts, those elements that reveal new insights and possibilities for healing.

Trauma theory will serve as the cornerstone of our exploration, illuminating the psychological, emotional, and relational complexities that male survivors endure. The "shiny object" in this context is the recognition that both the biological responses and cognitive distortions resulting from trauma are, in fact, psychologically normal adaptations to the individual's experiences. These responses, while adaptive to the survivor's specific context, are often perceived as maladaptive by society because the trauma-induced experiences are abnormal to the culture at large. By understanding how trauma reshapes the mind and spirit—distorting perceptions of self and others—we gain the power to help survivors rewrite their narratives, transforming what society views as maladaptive into sources of strength and resilience. This shift in perspective allows for a deeper, more compassionate approach to healing, where the very mechanisms that once seemed destructive are reframed as natural, albeit misunderstood, survival strategies.

Gender theory offers another critical facet to explore, revealing how societal norms and expectations shape male survivors' identities and influence their interactions. The "shiny object" in gender theory is the opportunity to challenge and dismantle the rigid constructs that often inhibit male survivors from fully expressing their vulnerabilities. This is particularly important in a therapeutic landscape where the majority of therapists are women, and much of the research and societal understanding tends to frame sexual trauma predominantly as a female experience. These dynamics can create additional barriers for male survivors, who may feel that their experiences are misunderstood or invalidated. By addressing these gendered dynamics, therapists can craft interventions that resonate more deeply with male survivors' unique experiences, fostering a space where they can reclaim their identities on their own terms and navigate their healing journey without the constraints of traditional gender expectations.

Attachment theory opens a window into the multifaceted nature of human relationships, emphasizing the profound impact of early relational experiences on individual development. The "shiny object" here is the understanding that while trauma occurs within the context of relationships, it is within relationships that healing must also occur. This realization goes beyond merely understanding attachment styles; it involves recognizing how these attachment patterns are shaped and influenced by the interplay of gender and trauma narratives. By examining attachment within this broader context, we gain the tools to not only understand how trauma disrupts relationships but also how we can rebuild trust, intimacy, and security in the lives of survivors. This approach empowers us to support survivors in forming healthy, fulfilling relationships, knowing that the path to healing is deeply embedded in the relational connections they rebuild.

For male survivors of sexual abuse, understanding the intersection of trauma, gender, and attachment theory is crucial to their healing process. Sexuality is often the entry point that brings many male survivors into treatment, as the trauma they've endured has profoundly violated and distorted their sexual development. Gender theory gives us a framework for understanding societal expectations placed on men, particularly in terms of sexuality, which can compound feelings of shame and confusion. These survivors are often caught in a conflict between what society expects of them as men and the internalized effects of their trauma. This tension complicates their sense of identity and their ability to navigate relationships, especially intimate ones.

A comprehensive understanding of **sexual development** enables therapists to recognize how interpersonal sexual trauma has disrupted the survivor's sexual template, impacting not only their sexuality but also their overall identity and relationships. The "shiny object" in this context represents the surface-level behaviors or issues—like sexual compulsivity, avoidance, or risky behaviors—that may appear to be the problem but are actually coping mechanisms tied to deeper, unresolved trauma. The real work lies in exploring how the survivor's sexual development was interrupted and distorted by the trauma, and in helping them rewrite what is normal for them, free from societal shame or judgment.

Shame and judgment are often internalized due to societal or cultural expectations about what it means to be a man. These expectations create additional layers of pressure for male survivors, leading them to believe they are somehow broken or defective because of their trauma. The process of healing, therefore, involves unpacking these internalized beliefs and helping survivors understand that their reactions—whether it be sexual behaviors, avoidance, or emotional dysregulation—are natural responses to the trauma they have experienced. These responses served an adaptive function at the time of the abuse, but they may no longer serve them in their present lives.

Understanding trauma within the lens of attachment theory further helps male survivors realize how their relationships, especially intimate ones, have been shaped by the abuse. Many male survivors struggle with forming secure attachments because the trauma has impacted their ability to trust and feel safe with others. These men may avoid intimacy, or alternatively, engage in compulsive sexual behaviors as a way to manage the unresolved trauma. Educating survivors about how trauma has affected their attachment styles helps them begin to recognize patterns in their relationships and gives them the tools to start healing from these attachment wounds.

Therapists play a pivotal role in guiding survivors through this complex process. By helping them explore the specific ways their sexual development has been disrupted, therapists allow survivors to reconnect with their sense of self in a way that is both empowering and affirming. The goal is to help survivors reclaim their sexual identity and their relationships, recognizing that their previous coping mechanisms—however destructive they may seem—were once essential for their survival.

Through a lens of curiosity rather than judgment, therapists can help survivors challenge the societal and cultural pressures that have shaped their views of masculinity, sexuality, and self-worth. This shift away from judgment creates space for survivors to explore their trauma without the burden of shame, allowing them to better understand how their trauma has shaped their behaviors and identities.

Ultimately, the goal is to create a framework for healing that acknowledges the unique impacts of their trauma while freeing them from the distortions imposed by shame and external judgment. Through this process, survivors can begin to make sense of their experiences and reclaim their sexuality, relationships, and sense of self in a way that aligns with their true identity, rather than the distorted narrative imposed by their trauma.

As we explore the concept of the shiny object, it's essential to understand the profound impact of trauma. Trauma theory, which originated in the field of psychology, has since been applied across various disciplines such as sociology, anthropology, and history. This theory is grounded in the understanding that trauma can have a significant and lasting impact on an individual's mental and physical health.

FUNCTION OF BEHAVIOR

Trauma theory identifies several common reactions to trauma, including post-traumatic stress disorder (PTSD), dissociation, and other mental health challenges like depression and anxiety. It also highlights the influence of social factors—such as gender, race, and class—on the experience and effects of trauma.

Trauma theory underscores the importance of social support and the critical role of a trauma-informed approach in aiding recovery. This approach emphasizes the need for compassionate, empathetic care that acknowledges the impact of trauma and actively works to address its effects on both individuals and communities.

There are three essential components to PTSD that are crucial for anyone with experience in trauma to understand: avoidance, compulsive repetition, and anxiety. By grasping these core principles, it becomes easier to recognize these behaviors and, if one chooses, explore how to manage them effectively.

It's also important to recognize that all behavior serves a function; there is always a reason why we do what we do. The primary and often the most critical lens through which we should examine this function is that of safety and protection. Safety and protection encompass both physical and psychological well-being. Therefore, when someone experiences trauma, these three components—avoidance, compulsive repetition, and anxiety—often serve as compensatory mechanisms to maintain a sense of safety.

In the mental health field, behaviors associated with PTSD are often pathologized, largely because our mental health system is rooted in a medical model that tends to label anything outside the norm as "sick" or disordered. Consequently, these behaviors are frequently viewed as pathological. However, by exploring these three functions through the lens of safety, we can better understand how they might actually serve a protective role for the individual in the context of their trauma.

As we continue to explore the reactions to trauma through a functional lens, it's crucial to recognize that one of the significant aspects of trauma is the cognitive distortions it creates. These distortions often reinforce the perception that one remains in an unsafe situation, making the maintenance of symptoms like avoidance, compulsive repetition, and anxiety feel necessary for survival. This is especially challenging in the context of interpersonal trauma, where the offender may use the relationship to manipulate and exploit the survivor, further deepening these distortions.

For survivors of relational trauma, these distortions are intricately tied to their experiences within relationships, making the risk of taking a "leap of faith" in their recovery process extraordinarily daunting. This leap is essential for healing, as it involves trusting again and stepping into vulnerability within the safety of a relationship. Therefore, it's vital for anyone in a relationship with a survivor of interpersonal trauma to understand how they can contribute to a healing environment.

When I refer to recovery, I mean no longer meeting the criteria for PTSD. However, it's important to acknowledge that because the need for safety is literally embedded in our DNA, we will continue to have reactions and triggers in certain situations. The key difference in recovery is the ability to slow down and pace ourselves, recognize these triggers, and seek validation—whether through another trusted person or by identifying additional data sources to verify the reality of what we're experiencing. This awareness and ability to manage triggers are critical components of long-term healing.

I strongly believe that full recovery from interpersonal trauma is possible if the individual is motivated and supported within a relationship that is safe enough to encourage this leap of faith. While "Beyond the Shiny Object" is primarily written for therapists, these principles are valuable for anyone seeking to show up effectively in relationships, offering the potential to be a source of healing for those who have experienced relational trauma.

Chapter 4

UNRAVELLING THE IMPACT: EXPLORING TRAUMA THEORY IN DEPTH

In this chapter, we will delve into the fundamental elements of PTSD as identified by the DSM V; Avoidance, Anxiety, and Compulsive Repetition—and uncover the "shiny objects" within each. These shiny objects represent the deeper insights and critical nuances that can lead to more effective understanding and healing. We will also explore a central aspect of interpersonal trauma, what Judith Herman refers to as Complex Post-Traumatic Stress Disorder (C-PTSD). Herman's concept of C-PTSD expands upon the traditional understanding of PTSD by shining a light on the impact on the nervous system and the resulting cognitive distortions. By examining these elements closely, we will reveal the essential truths that can guide both survivors and therapists toward more profound recovery and resilience.

Avoidance is a common and often necessary coping mechanism for individuals who have experienced trauma. The overwhelming memories and emotions associated with the traumatic event can be so intense that steering clear of them feels like the only way to maintain a sense of stability. In this context, avoidance becomes the "shiny object"—a seemingly helpful tool that captures the survivor's focus, offering temporary relief by distracting from the painful reality of the trauma. However, while this shiny object provides short-term comfort, it also becomes the primary feature that inhibits true healing. By continually evading the painful memories and emotions, individuals prevent themselves from fully processing their trauma, which ultimately hinders their long-term well-being and recovery. Over time, this reliance on avoidance can create a cycle that perpetuates the very distress it seeks to escape, making it essential to gradually shift focus from the shiny object of avoidance to confronting and integrating these experiences in order to achieve genuine healing.

The metaphor of the "shiny object" can be a powerful tool in helping individuals understand this phenomenon and encouraging them to address their trauma in a healthy and productive manner. This metaphor illustrates how avoidance behaviors can divert attention away from the underlying issues that need healing. By recognizing and actively working to overcome these avoidance patterns, individuals can begin to process their trauma and move toward genuine recovery.

The "shiny object" metaphor describes how trauma survivors might avoid processing their traumatic experiences by focusing on seemingly attractive or engaging distractions. Just as someone might be drawn to a shiny object, they might fixate on certain activities or tasks, rather than addressing the deeper, unresolved emotions. This metaphor highlights the way in which avoidance can serve as a coping strategy, effectively masking the underlying distress.

This avoidance can manifest in various forms, such as excelling in sports, work, or other activities. By immersing themselves in these pursuits, individuals create a buffer against the painful experiences they wish to forget. However, understanding and addressing this dynamic is crucial for moving beyond avoidance and toward meaningful healing.

Let's explore how avoidance functions within the context of PTSD and its connection to the metaphor of the "shiny object." Avoidance is a common response among trauma survivors, often manifesting as a way to prevent the painful emotions and memories associated with their trauma from surfacing. Aron (2019) delves deeper into this concept by examining how perfectionism plays a role in the lives of trauma survivors. These individuals may become intensely focused on specific tasks or skills, intertwining their identity with their achievements to fend off intrusive traumatic memories.

For trauma survivors, overwhelming emotions and memories can be difficult to manage, and avoidance becomes a method of maintaining control over their inner world. The "shiny object" serves as a distraction, capturing their attention and providing a sense of accomplishment and control. For instance, a trauma survivor might channel their energy into becoming a top athlete. The rigorous training, discipline, and focus required for sports create a structured environment where the individual can excel. The accolades and recognition they receive reinforce their identity, making their achievements central to their self-worth. However, this intense focus on sports also serves as a powerful distraction from the unresolved trauma. The physical exertion and mental concentration leave little room for intrusive thoughts, effectively pushing the trauma to the background.

Similarly, in the workplace, a trauma survivor might become a workaholic, dedicating long hours and immense effort to their job. Professional success and praise provide a sense of identity and validation. Work becomes a sanctuary where they can escape the chaos of their internal world. However, this hyperfocus on work can lead to burnout and further emotional distress if not balanced with self-care and processing of the underlying trauma.

The danger of this form of avoidance lies in its unsustainability. The "shiny object" can only distract for so long before the unresolved trauma resurfaces, often more intensely. Additionally, the individual may become overly reliant on their achievements for self-worth, leading to a fragile sense of identity that is vulnerable to failure or setbacks.

Substituting the desire to avoid trauma with a "shiny object" is a complex and often insidious form of avoidance. While it may result in impressive achievements and external validation, it ultimately hinders the healing process by diverting attention from the underlying trauma. Recognizing and addressing this pattern is essential for trauma survivors to achieve genuine healing and develop a balanced sense of self.

NAVIGATING THE SHADOWS: EXPLORING THE FUNCTIONS OF AVOIDANCE IN TRAUMA

FOOD

A clear example of a "shiny object" in the context of avoidance is disordered eating. Disordered eating affects both men and women, but it's often perceived differently across genders, with much of the focus traditionally on females. This highlights how eating behaviors can serve dual functions as a coping mechanism in the context of avoidance.

When examining the role of disordered eating as a shiny object, it's evident that, for some men, gaining weight and becoming larger is perceived as a way to project strength and invulnerability. This physical transformation can reduce the perceived risk of being harmed again, as increased size and a more intimidating appearance create a protective barrier. Additionally, weight gain might make them less attractive to potential offenders, further enhancing this sense of safety. In this way, disordered eating serves as a form of avoidance, allowing men to control how they are perceived and to create a sense of security through their physical appearance.

Another significant function of food in the context of avoidance is its connection to the brain's reward system. Certain foods, particularly those high in carbohydrates, trigger a dopamine response that temporarily alleviates emotional distress. For trauma survivors, food can become a source of comfort and a means to numb emotional pain. The act of eating, especially foods that provide a quick dopamine rush, offers short-term relief from anxiety and depression. However, this reliance on food to regulate emotions can lead to an addiction, where eating becomes a way to avoid dealing with traumatic memories.

Disordered eating patterns, such as binge eating, serve as a distraction from the distressing thoughts and feelings associated with trauma. The intense focus on food and eating behaviors can keep the mind preoccupied, preventing the intrusion of traumatic memories. However, this avoidance strategy comes at a significant cost. Over time, disordered eating can lead to severe physical and psychological health problems, including obesity, diabetes, heart disease, and increased emotional distress.

While food may act as a shiny object that helps trauma survivors avoid confronting their pain, it ultimately perpetuates a cycle of avoidance that hinders healing and leads to further complications. Recognizing this pattern is crucial for addressing the underlying trauma and fostering long-term recovery.

SUBSTANCE USE

One of the most prevalent forms of avoidance that men present in treatment is substance use. While we will explore this topic in greater depth later in the book, it is essential to address its role in avoidance now. Substance use often serves as a shiny object for men dealing with trauma—a way to distract from and temporarily escape their emotional pain. Beyond mere avoidance, substance use also fulfills a deep-seated need for belonging, especially in communities that society might view as deviant or flawed. This perpetuates the internalized belief that many survivors of interpersonal sexual abuse hold—that they are somehow defective and therefore only truly belong with others who are similarly "defective."

Research has shown that men are more likely to turn to substance use as a coping mechanism following sexual trauma compared to women. While women more commonly report depression in response to trauma, men often gravitate toward substance use as a means of avoiding their emotional pain and reinforcing a socially constructed image of toughness and resilience. This behavior is not only about avoiding the pain; it's also about finding a place where they feel they belong, even if that place is within a group that society views as less than.

The shared experience of substance use creates a sense of camaraderie and understanding among men who feel disconnected from mainstream society. For many, these environments offer the only sense of belonging they have, even though the behaviors that unite them are self-destructive. The societal perception of those who engage in substance use as deviant only reinforces the belief that they are defective, further entrenching their reliance on these communities.

This need for belonging extends even into recovery. In many 12-step programs, the identity of "I am an addict" provides a new form of belonging—a community where individuals share struggles and a commitment to sobriety. However, the intense focus on maintaining sobriety can sometimes become another form of the shiny object—an outward goal that distracts from addressing the deeper, underlying issues that led to substance use in the first place. While the achievement of sobriety is undoubtedly crucial, especially for individuals with a compulsive nature where avoiding substance use is essential for good mental health, it can also serve as a way to avoid exploring the root causes of the addiction.

By concentrating solely on not using the substance, individuals may bypass the necessary work of understanding the trauma, emotions, and patterns that initially drove them to substance use. This focus on sobriety, while beneficial in preventing relapse, can sometimes perpetuate the avoidance of deeper healing. The 12-step model offers invaluable support and a pathway to recovery, but it also highlights the complex interplay between identity, belonging, and the need to confront underlying psychological wounds.

In this context, sobriety itself can become a shiny object—an important achievement that, if not accompanied by deeper therapeutic work, may leave the core issues unresolved. It is essential for recovery to include not just the cessation of substance use, but also a thorough exploration of the function that substance use served, allowing individuals to address the underlying trauma and emotional pain that continues to impact their lives.

For men who adopt hypermasculine behaviors as a means of coping with trauma, substance use can serve as a way to project strength and toughness. This allows them to avoid confronting vulnerabilities by rejecting any sign of weakness. Yet, this strategy comes at a significant cost. By clinging to substance use and hypermasculinity, they often delay or avoid seeking help, as doing so would require them to face the very vulnerabilities they are trying to suppress.

In contrast, women who experience trauma may more readily seek help or express their emotions, leading to different coping strategies and recovery paths. Understanding these gender differences is crucial for developing effective interventions.

Ultimately, substance use and hypermasculinity serve as barriers to recovery, preventing men from engaging in the healing process. Mental health professionals must recognize the ways in which avoidance, the need for belonging, and societal gender norms intersect, creating strategies that encourage men to embrace vulnerability and seek help. By fostering a healthier, more balanced expression of masculinity, we can support men in their journey toward healing, helping them to find belonging in communities that promote growth and recovery rather than perpetuating a cycle of avoidance and pain.

THRILL-SEEKING BEHAVIORS

In the realm of hypervigilance, another form of avoidance intertwined with anxiety for men emerges—the fight response. For trauma survivors, especially those constantly on high alert, the mind is perpetually scanning for threats, interpreting even minor provocations as potential dangers. This heightened state of readiness serves as a way to avoid the feelings of helplessness and fear that often accompany trauma. Maintaining this state of vigilance feels necessary—a form of avoidance that offers a sense of control in a world that seems perpetually unsafe.

For some men, this need for control manifests in the pursuit of high-adrenaline activities—driving recklessly, skydiving, or engaging in extreme sports. These behaviors serve a dual purpose: they offer an escape from the pervasive sense of fear while also allowing men to assert control over their environment. The thrill of speeding down a highway at dangerous speeds, jumping out of an airplane, or pushing the limits in extreme sports provides a temporary reprieve from the anxieties lurking beneath the surface. These activities offer more than just a rush; they provide a fleeting sense of invincibility and power.

In this context, the pursuit of these adrenaline-fueled activities becomes a shiny object—a distraction that momentarily masks the underlying fear and trauma. Whether it's the thrill of dodging traffic at high speeds or the rush of freefalling from thousands of feet, these activities offer a way to feel alive and in control, even if only for a moment. However, this relentless chase for the next thrill, while it may appear to embody toughness and strength, ultimately serves as a distraction from the deeper work of healing. The line between calculated risk and genuine danger becomes blurred, as the need to conquer fear through these intense experiences overshadows the need to address the root causes of that fear.

DISSOCIATION

On the other side of hypervigilance lies hypo-vigilance, a state often described as drifting on a foggy sea where the world feels distant and muted. This diminished alertness and awareness is closely tied to the freeze response, a form of dissociation that functions as a means of avoidance. Imagine walking through a bustling marketplace, but instead of being engaged by the vibrant sights and sounds, you feel detached, as if observing everything from behind a thick pane of glass. In this dissociative state, the senses become dulled, and the world appears stripped of its color and vitality—a "shiny object" that distracts and numbs, offering an escape from overwhelming emotions.

Physiologically, hypo-vigilance manifests in various ways. Muscles feel heavy and lethargic, as if weighed down by an invisible burden. The heart beats slowly, lacking the urgency and intensity of its hypervigilant counterpart. Breathing becomes shallow and labored, as if even the act of existing requires more effort than it should.

This state of dissociation also profoundly impacts the mind. Thoughts drift like clouds across a hazy sky, fragmented and disjointed—another example of behavior functioning to avoid pain. Concentration becomes a Herculean task, as if trying to grasp fleeting memories that slip through your fingers like grains of sand. Emotions, once vivid and raw, seem distant and inaccessible, locked away behind a heavy door.

Yet within this fog of hypo-vigilance lies the allure of a "shiny object," a form of avoidance that provides a sense of calm. Dissociation, while it obscures the world, offers a temporary refuge from the relentless barrage of stimuli that often accompanies hypervigilance. This avoidance strategy functions as a sanctuary, a quiet escape where the mind can retreat from chaos. However, just like any shiny object, this sense of calm is fleeting and deceptive, masking deeper issues that must eventually be faced to fully engage with and process life's challenges.

Treating this form of avoidance can be particularly challenging because the very essence of dissociation is avoidance itself. It is an incredibly adaptive response, often intertwined with a man's sense of resilience and survival. For many, dissociation has been a vital tool, helping them navigate overwhelming situations and emotions. It feeds into the hypermasculine concept of stoicism—the idea that real men don't show vulnerability or distress, but instead maintain a stoic, composed exterior regardless of inner turmoil. This stoicism is often admired and accepted by others as a sign of manliness, further reinforcing the dissociative coping mechanism as both effective and socially acceptable.

Recognizing this coping mechanism as problematic can be difficult, as it is deeply ingrained and often seen as a strength rather than a barrier to healing. Integrating the idea that this shiny object, while adaptive, may also be hindering their recovery, requires a delicate and nuanced therapeutic approach, one that honors their resilience while gently guiding them toward a more integrated and engaged way of being. In this way, therapy becomes not just about managing symptoms, but about challenging deeply held beliefs about what it means to be strong, to be a man, and to heal.

FAWN RESPONSE

Another aspect of hypo-vigilance is the fawn response, where the instinct to appease and placate aggressors takes center stage, especially in the face of overwhelming threats. Imagine standing before a towering wave, knowing you can't outrun or withstand its force. Instead, you bow your head, bend your knees, and hope it will pass without crashing down on you. This response is deeply rooted in the need to prioritize safety, a survival mechanism that seeks to avoid harm at all costs.

For men, particularly those who have experienced trauma or abuse, the fawn response can become a familiar strategy—a learned behavior that ensures survival in treacherous situations. This behavior acts as a "shiny object," offering a temporary sense of security by focusing on immediate safety and deflecting attention from deeper, unresolved issues.

In the business world, the fawn response can be particularly adaptive, manifesting as a need to maintain control by subtly manipulating others. It might involve excessive agreement or offering concessions not out of genuine belief but as a calculated tactic to avoid conflict and secure a deal. This approach often shifts the focus from finding a truly beneficial solution to placating the other party, sometimes at the expense of one's own interests or integrity.

This strategy can be highly effective in the short term, creating an illusion of harmony and cooperation. In a world that often equates masculinity with the ability to control outcomes and avoid vulnerability, the fawn response can seem like a powerful tool. It allows men to navigate complex social interactions and business negotiations while maintaining an image of strength and competence.

However, this manipulation can ultimately undermine long-term success. The lack of sincerity in these interactions may lead to imbalanced agreements that fail to address the true needs of either party. Over time, the fawn response can erode trust and breed resentment, as it becomes clear that the behavior was more about manipulation than genuine collaboration.

In essence, the fawn response in this context functions as a way to survive by avoiding direct confrontation or disagreement. Yet, like the "shiny object," it offers only a superficial solution, masking the deeper issues that need to be addressed for a truly successful and sustainable outcome. While this approach may be adaptive and even admired in certain circles, it can also prevent the development of authentic relationships and solutions that endure beyond the immediate crisis.

UNSEEN WOUNDS: ANXIETY AND THE BIOLOGICAL IMPACT OF TRAUMA

The second element that we will investigate relating to PTSD is **Anxiety**. Trauma can profoundly affect the brain, particularly in areas crucial for emotional processing and regulation. The experience of trauma can lead to significant changes in how the brain functions, influencing an individual's emotional responses, memory, and behavior. Understanding these changes through the lens of safety is essential when considering the function of behaviors and determining the most effective interventions for managing emotional responses.

The amygdala, a critical region of the brain responsible for processing emotional information and detecting threats, often becomes hyperactive in individuals who have experienced trauma. This hyperactivity leads to an exaggerated fear response and heightened anxiety, as the amygdala continues to signal danger even in relatively safe situations. This behavior is rooted in the brain's survival mechanism—keeping the individual alert to potential threats, even when the actual danger has passed. As a result, the nervous system remains in a state of heightened alert, which can lead to chronic anxiety and significant difficulties in forming and maintaining relationships.

Trauma also impacts the prefrontal cortex, the part of the brain responsible for regulating emotions and making decisions. Trauma can decrease activity in this area, impairing an individual's ability to regulate emotions and make sound decisions. When the prefrontal cortex is compromised, top-down approaches to emotional regulation—such as cognitive strategies that involve reappraisal or reframing—become less effective. This impairment leaves individuals more dependent on bottom-up approaches, which are based on physiological and sensory interventions to manage emotional responses.

The hippocampus, which plays a crucial role in memory processing, is another area of the brain affected by trauma. Traumatic experiences can cause difficulties in remembering certain aspects of the event, leading to flashbacks and intrusive memories. These memory-related symptoms are often triggered by specific cues or reminders, which can activate the amygdala and lead to a heightened state of arousal. In such cases, bottom-up approaches to emotional regulation, which focus on altering physiological states, may be particularly effective in managing the intense emotional responses triggered by these memories.

Understanding the interplay between the amygdala and the prefrontal cortex in the context of trauma is crucial for developing effective therapeutic strategies. The amygdala, which is responsible for processing emotions and detecting threats, can become dysregulated due to trauma. This dysregulation can manifest in two primary ways: hyperactivity or hypoactivity. When the amygdala is overactive, it floods the nervous system with signals of danger, causing the prefrontal cortex—responsible for reasoning and decision-making—to become overwhelmed. In this state, the prefrontal cortex shifts into a heightened safety-seeking mode, losing its ability to analyze information rationally and make thoughtful decisions.

On the other hand, when the amygdala is underactive, it creates a state of freeze or hypoarousal. In this case, the prefrontal cortex is effectively "shut down" and unable to interpret cues from the body accurately. The individual may feel emotionally numb or detached, as their body remains frozen in a survival response.

Without recognizing how a specific trigger is impacting the nervous system—whether by over-arousing it or causing it to shut down—the therapist may inadvertently choose interventions that do not align with the client's needs in the moment. This can slow the recovery process and hinder emotional regulation.

The direct correlation between the dysregulation of the amygdala and the impaired functioning of the prefrontal cortex makes it essential for therapists to assess the state of the nervous system during therapy. By doing so, they can adjust their approach accordingly, either calming an overactive nervous system or helping to awaken a hypoactive one, allowing the client to engage more effectively in the healing process.

In a hypo-response, where the nervous system is underactive and frozen, a bottom-up approach is essential. This strategy focuses on altering the physiological and sensory experiences that underlie emotional responses, which are crucial when the prefrontal cortex is disengaged due to a trauma-induced shutdown. In such cases, the body is not receiving or interpreting cues properly, and the individual may feel numb or detached. Bottom-up interventions like deep breathing, mindfulness, or physical exercise help reawaken the body's connection to safety by regulating physiological arousal. For example, deep breathing slows the heart rate, bringing the nervous system out of its frozen state and allowing the individual to begin re-engaging with their environment. These approaches work by calming the body first, which in turn helps the mind start processing emotions more effectively.

In contrast, during a hyper-response, when the nervous system is overactive and in a state of heightened arousal, a top-down approach becomes more effective. In this state, the prefrontal cortex is overwhelmed by the flood of danger signals from the amygdala, leading to intense safety-seeking behaviors and a reduced capacity for rational thought. Top-down interventions focus on cognitive strategies to re-engage the prefrontal cortex and help the individual regain control over their emotional responses. For instance, by reframing a stressful situation—such as viewing a challenge as an opportunity for growth rather than a potential failure—an individual can reduce anxiety and regain perspective. This cognitive reappraisal requires an active prefrontal cortex and helps shift focus from immediate, emotional responses to more logical, thoughtful problem-solving.

By understanding whether the individual is experiencing a hypo or hyper response, therapists can tailor their interventions accordingly, using bottom-up strategies to regulate an underactive nervous system and top-down strategies to calm an overactive one. This balance is essential for helping trauma survivors regain control over their emotional and cognitive responses.

The ultimate goal in addressing trauma is to create equilibrium between the cognitive (the way the mind thinks) and the somatic (the way the body feels) with the external reality of the real world. Achieving this balance often requires choosing between top-down and bottom-up approaches, depending on the specific circumstances and triggers an individual faces. For instance, when someone feels overwhelmed by physiological symptoms of anxiety—such as a racing heart or shallow breathing—a bottom-up intervention may be more effective. This could involve grounding techniques or sensory modulation to calm the body's stress response, aligning the physical state with the external environment.

Conversely, when negative thought patterns or catastrophic thinking drive the emotional response, a top-down approach might be more suitable. This method involves cognitive strategies, such as reappraisal or reframing, to adjust the mental interpretation of events, thereby helping the mind align with reality.

Behavior in response to trauma is intricately linked to the individual's biological response to perceived threats. Both top-down and bottom-up approaches aim to restore a sense of safety by bringing the mind and body into harmony with the external world. These interventions must be tailored to the specific circumstances and triggers an individual encounters. The most effective approach often combines both strategies, addressing the mind and body simultaneously. This dual focus helps individuals navigate their triggers, facilitating a journey toward healing that integrates cognitive and somatic experiences with the real world, making the process feel both safe and manageable.

INTEGRATING THE TRAUMA NARRATIVE: UNDERSTANDING AVOIDANCE, ANXIETY, AND BIOLOGICAL RESPONSES IN JOHN'S STORY

John's story, as we've begun to explore, reveals a man who, on the surface, has achieved everything society deems successful. He's reached the pinnacle of his field, a place where many would find satisfaction and contentment. But for John, it was never enough. Each success, each accolade, was just another shiny object, another distraction from the deep-seated pain and shame that had followed him from childhood. The more he achieved, the more he strove, not out of ambition alone, but out of a desperate need to keep the darkness at bay.

John's success was not merely a product of hard work and intelligence—it was also deeply rooted in his hypervigilance and the fawning response, both of which had been ingrained in him as survival mechanisms from his early experiences of interpersonal sexual trauma. His hypervigilance allowed him to read a room with uncanny precision, to anticipate the needs and moods of others, and to navigate complex social and business landscapes with ease. This heightened state of alertness, while exhausting, became one of his most valuable tools in the business world. It gave him an edge, but it also kept him in a constant state of readiness, always scanning for threats, always preparing for the worst.

The fawning response, another byproduct of his trauma, manifested in his ability to charm and appease those around him. John knew how to make people feel at ease, how to say the right things, how to present himself as exactly what they wanted him to be. This made him highly effective in negotiations and relationship-building, essential skills for a businessman. But this ability to fawn, to mold himself to others' expectations, came at a cost. It often left him feeling disconnected from his own needs and desires, further reinforcing his sense of defectiveness and the belief that his worth was tied to his ability to please others.

As he climbed higher in his career, the sense of accomplishment that once came with his achievements began to wane. The thrill of sealing a big deal, the satisfaction of outmaneuvering a competitor— these victories that had once filled the void within him were no longer enough. The shiny objects that had served as distractions for so long were losing their luster. And as they did, the heaviness of his sense of defectiveness, the monster within that he had tried so hard to suppress, began to invade his mind more and more.

This is the paradox of John's success: the more he accomplished, the less satisfied he became. What once provided a sense of control and validation now felt hollow, leaving him increasingly vulnerable to the very feelings of worthlessness he had been running from all his life. The monster of shame, the deep-rooted belief that he was fundamentally flawed because of his past, grew stronger as his achievements lost their power to distract him from it.

John's relentless pursuit of success was never about the success itself; it was about the avoidance of pain. But as he reached the pinnacle of his career, the distractions became less effective, and the avoidance less possible. The shiny objects that had once served him so well were failing to keep the darkness at bay, and the unresolved trauma of his past was demanding to be addressed.

His hypervigilance, once a tool for success, became a source of constant anxiety. His fawning, once a strategy for building alliances, started to feel like a betrayal of his true self. The very mechanisms that had helped him survive and succeed were now contributing to his unraveling.

In therapy, this realization was a turning point. John had to confront the truth that his achievements, while impressive, were not enough to silence the monster within. The sense of defectiveness, the shame that had driven so much of his life, was not something he could outrun or out-achieve. It was something he had to face head-on.

The challenge for John was not just in recognizing this pattern but in understanding that the path to healing lay not in more success, but in embracing the vulnerability he had always feared. It was about moving beyond the shiny objects, the distractions, and beginning the difficult work of integrating his experiences into a coherent narrative of self-acceptance and growth.

For John, and for many like him, the journey to healing required a fundamental shift in perspective. It required him to stop looking outward for validation and start looking inward for understanding. It required him to see that the monster within was not something to be feared or avoided, but something to be understood and integrated. Only then could he begin to find the peace and satisfaction that had eluded him for so long.

CYCLES OF REPETITION: UNRAVELING THE CONNECTION BETWEEN TRAUMA AND RECURRENT BEHAVIORS

Repetition is the third and final element we explore, particularly in how it intertwines with hyperarousal to create a continuous cycle where survivors repeatedly relive their traumatic experiences. This cycle often distorts reality, making individuals feel as though the original threat is occurring in the present moment. This distortion, rooted in the trauma itself, can make relationships particularly challenging, as the trauma frequently originated within a relational context. Specific elements of the traumatic event can be replayed over and over, reinforcing the survivor's sense of danger and vulnerability.

This heightened state of alertness, or hyperarousal, seeps into everyday life, manifesting in behaviors such as irritability, difficulty concentrating, and an exaggerated startle response. The trauma echoes through intrusive thoughts, nightmares, and flashbacks, leading to emotional dysregulation and complicating the survivor's ability to maintain a sense of normalcy.

These repetitive behaviors, directly linked to the original trauma, can persist throughout a person's life unless they are actively addressed and resolved. They are manifestations of the long-lasting impact of trauma, serving as a coping mechanism that, while offering a false sense of safety, often distorts the individual's perception of reality. For instance, hyperarousal can lead to situations where someone might look out a window and mistakenly believe the perpetrator is outside when it's merely a harmless object, like a set of bushes. This constant state of vigilance may provide temporary relief from the perceived threat but ultimately prevents the individual from truly feeling safe.

THE FUNCTION OF BEHAVIOR IN SEXUALITY: REPETITION AND SAFETY-SEEKING

One of the primary reasons many men come into treatment is the impact of their sexual behavior on their relationships. When we explore the function of behavior as it relates to sexuality, it's crucial to understand how these behaviors are often rooted in safety-seeking mechanisms, especially in the context of trauma. As previously mentioned, one of the core elements of PTSD is compulsive repetition. Since this book focuses on interpersonal trauma, it's essential to consider how repetition plays out in the lives of survivors.

Repetition can manifest in various ways, and one of the most direct forms is reenacting behaviors related to the original trauma. The theory behind this is that by repeatedly engaging in behaviors that mirror the traumatic experience, the individual is attempting to gain control over the unresolved emotions and dynamics tied to that event. For many men, this shows up in their sexual behavior, particularly in their consumption of certain types of pornography or in engaging with partners in ways that mimic the trauma narrative. It's important to recognize that the repetition itself is not always about sex—sexuality can be a "shiny object" masking deeper dynamics related to the trauma.

For example, men who frequently use sex workers may not just be seeking physical satisfaction but also recreating the transactional nature of the abuse they endured. The ability to control the terms of the interaction, from payment to setting boundaries, may mirror the way they interpreted the power dynamics of their trauma. In these cases, sex becomes a form of control, a way to keep emotional vulnerability at bay while maintaining a familiar, albeit dysfunctional, narrative. This repetition is less about sexuality itself and more about reenacting the dynamics of control and power that were present in their trauma.

Another way this repetitive behavior can show up is through engaging in sexual relationships outside the agreed-upon boundaries of a committed relationship. This breach of the relational "contract" is often a way for men to emotionally disengage from their partners, using avoidance as a way to protect themselves from true intimacy. In this case, the behavior is not just about seeking physical pleasure but avoiding the emotional vulnerability that comes with being fully present in a relationship. Additionally, this can have elements of self-sabotage, as cheating gives the individual an excuse to end the relationship on their terms, avoiding the possibility of being abandoned by their partner.

In all these examples, we see how the repetition of trauma-related dynamics can be hidden beneath the surface of sexual behavior, with sexuality itself acting as a shiny object that distracts from the underlying emotional drivers. Later in this section, we will delve into the concept of the circle of sexuality and how specific sexual templates are formed for men, influenced by trauma. Understanding these templates is essential for helping male survivors reclaim a healthier sense of sexuality and intimacy, free from the compulsive repetition that once controlled their behavior.

In some cases, repetition manifests in more complex, subtle behaviors that are harder to decipher. These behaviors are intricately connected to the trauma response and often reflect unresolved aspects of past experiences. While thrill-seeking behaviors may offer a socially acceptable outlet for managing anxiety and reinforce a sense of control, other repetitive behaviors operate on a deeper, more unconscious level, perpetuating the cycle of trauma and making it difficult for survivors to break free from their past.

Let's consider an example of repetition in the context of interpersonal sexual trauma. A gay man, whom we'll call Tom, came to my office after facing recurring issues in his long-term relationship with his husband, Richard. Tom and Richard have been together for over 20 years and have always had an open relationship, with clear rules requiring that they notify each other if they engage in sexual activity outside the relationship. However, Tom compulsively avoids telling Richard about these encounters, despite the agreement they both have in place.

Richard's sense of betrayal stems not from the sexual activity itself—something they've mutually agreed upon—but from the lack of transparency and the embarrassment of learning about these encounters from other sources. Richard feels hurt and confused, struggling to understand why Tom, despite the established rules, repeatedly hides these interactions.

When we examined this behavior through the lens of Tom's trauma narrative, a deeper pattern emerged. Tom revealed that as a young teenager, he was involved in a sexual relationship with a man in his thirties. Although Tom initially did not perceive this as abuse—believing that he was gay and enjoyed the sexual activity—he eventually recognized that the secrecy surrounding the relationship was significant. He understood that the adults in his life would have seen the relationship as deeply inappropriate, not only because of his young age but also due to the significant power differential between them.

As Tom explored these past experiences in therapy, he began to see that the secrecy required in his teenage relationship was a form of compulsive repetition linked to his trauma. Although it took time for Tom to recognize that this relationship constituted sexual trauma, he eventually understood that his compulsion to keep secrets, even within a context where openness was explicitly agreed upon, was a way of reenacting the dynamics of his earlier trauma.

This realization allowed Tom to become curious about the patterns in his behavior, leading him to reexamine the impact of that early relationship on his current life. By acknowledging the repetitive nature of his secrecy, Tom could start to understand it as a coping mechanism born out of his past trauma—an attempt to exert control in a situation where he once felt powerless and vulnerable. This insight marked a significant step in his healing journey, allowing him to explore the deeper emotional currents that shaped his behavior and to work towards greater honesty and transparency in his relationship with Richard.

Repetition, as seen in Tom's story, often involves recreating elements of past trauma in the present, even when those behaviors no longer serve the individual's best interests. Recognizing these patterns is crucial for healing, as it opens the door to understanding how past trauma continues to influence current behaviors and relationships. Through this awareness, individuals like Tom can begin to break the cycle of compulsive repetition and move towards healthier, more fulfilling ways of relating to themselves and others.

I believe that repetition is the most essential element in helping men understand how their past experiences interplay with the difficulties they face in the present. This recognition can be the key to unlocking their curiosity, allowing them to connect the past with the present. Due to gender norms, many men are reluctant to explore their past or engage with difficult emotions, often avoiding these aspects altogether. However, by drawing their attention to the repetitive nature of their behaviors, they can often see the connection between past trauma and current challenges, which can be a powerful motivator for deeper exploration.

Let me share another example to illustrate this point. Brett, a man in his early 60s, had been married for almost 40 years and had always felt safe and connected with his wife. Despite this, he often struggled with feelings of disconnection from the world and a pervasive lack of joy. Brett had always remembered a traumatic experience from his childhood, but it wasn't until his thirties, after reading an article about a mass shooting, that these memories resurfaced with intense clarity, plunging him into a deep depression marked by anhedonia.

Brett knew that his past was playing a role in his current struggles, but he couldn't quite connect the dots. He had been in and out of therapy for years since this memory, yet intrusive thoughts continued to haunt him. During our sessions, Brett shared a story that seemed to hold the key to his repetitive behaviors. He recalled an incident from his childhood when he was at a friend's house. They were involved in a club together, led by the friend's father. On one particular occasion, the father tied Brett and his friend up and forced them to put their genitals in each other's mouths. The overwhelming feeling Brett experienced during this event was the fear that he was going to kill his friend by drowning him.

Given the nature of Brett's fear, I asked him if he had ever had any problems with urination. Startled by the question, Brett was visibly surprised, as if a forgotten memory had suddenly resurfaced. He then recounted how, as a young man, he had an obsessive need to void his bladder. He would empty his bladder before leaving the house and, when in public, would compulsively locate and use bathrooms on an hourly basis. This behavior had persisted for several years, driven by an intense, irrational fear.

As we explored this further, Brett immediately saw the connection between the traumatic experience with his friend and his compulsive behavior around urination. While this realization was distressing, it also provided a profound sense of relief. Brett finally understood the function of his behavior, validating the memories he had long doubted. This single insight allowed him to explore these thoughts not with fear and doubt, but with curiosity and a renewed sense of purpose.

By recognizing the repetitive nature of his behavior, Brett was able to see how his trauma had shaped his actions over the years. This understanding gave him the clarity he needed to explore his past more deeply and to address the root causes of his current struggles. In Brett's case, as in many others, repetition proved to be the key that unlocked the door to healing, enabling him to confront his trauma with a sense of curiosity rather than avoidance.

Repetition is a keystone in keeping men engaged in treatment, especially since many men struggle to seek out therapy on their own and often do so at the urging of others or because of a problem that seems unrelated to their sexual trauma. In the initial phase of treatment, my goal is to help men see past the "shiny object" and explore what lies beneath—unlocking the answers that can help them manage their behaviors more effectively. The compulsive nature of repetition related to trauma offers men an opportunity to understand that they are not "crazy" but are reacting to situations that have deeply impacted them. Once they find meaning in these patterns, their ability to manage them increases significantly.

One final example, let's revisit the story of John, who came to my office after being caught soliciting sex workers by his wife. As we explored his history, we identified two key functions of his current behaviors that were directly related to his sexual trauma. The first involved what he would ask the sex workers to do. In his trauma narrative, John was forced to perform oral sex on his stepfather—a secretive and powerless situation that deeply affected him. When we discussed his encounters with sex workers, John revealed that the only thing he would ask them to do was to provide oral sex. Although these connections were not made immediately, I was able to guide John to see the pattern of behavior that linked his trauma with his current actions. He even acknowledged that oral sex was something his wife was unwilling to do, which further reinforced its compulsive nature.

John also realized that whenever his life felt out of control—whether in business, fatherhood, or his relationship with his wife—the compulsion to seek out sex workers became overwhelming. Despite not wanting to engage in these behaviors, the sense of relief he experienced when he did so kept him trapped in this cycle. Like other compulsive behaviors that are misaligned with one's values, John felt tremendous guilt afterward, which led him to further isolate himself.

As we delved deeper into his behavior, John recognized that he felt a sense of control over the sex workers—control that he had lacked during his traumatic experiences with his stepfather. With the sex workers, he could entirely focus on his own needs and had complete control over when and how the encounters would occur, a stark contrast to the helplessness he felt as a child. Recognizing this, John could see that this, too, was a form of compulsive repetition.

Acknowledging the connection between the "shiny object" and the traumatic event initially provided John with a sense of relief, helping him to see that his behavior was not random but deeply rooted in his past experiences. The real breakthrough, however, came when he recognized that his compulsive actions were driven by a need for control, particularly when his life felt chaotic or overwhelming. This insight allowed John to understand the function of his behavior—not as a sign of being deviant or inherently unfaithful to his wife, but as a misguided attempt to regain a sense of power and control through sexual encounters.

By identifying alternative ways to perceive and establish control—through top-down interventions—John began to see a path forward that didn't involve destructive behaviors. This realization was empowering; it reframed his actions in a way that allowed him to view himself with more compassion and less self-condemnation. Understanding that his actions were rooted in a need to cope with feelings of powerlessness opened the door for John to explore healthier ways to manage his emotions, his relationships, and his life, moving beyond the cycle of control and manipulation that had previously dominated his actions.

BEYOND PTSD: A CLOSER LOOK AT THE COMPLEXITIES OF COMPLEX POST-TRAUMATIC STRESS DISORDER

In 1992, Judith Herman, a pioneering figure in trauma psychology, introduced the concept of Complex Post-Traumatic Stress Disorder (C-PTSD). Her groundbreaking work highlighted the deep connection between C-PTSD and childhood traumas, emphasizing the lasting impact that early life experiences can have on an individual's psychological well-being. Herman's contributions have been increasingly recognized, with C-PTSD gaining further validation through its inclusion in the World Health Organization's International Classification of Diseases (ICD-11) in 2022.

Herman's work was pivotal in recognizing the interplay between the three core aspects of PTSD—avoidance, anxiety, and compulsive repetition—and how these elements manifest in those who have experienced interpersonal trauma. Long before the full understanding of the biological impact of trauma on the nervous system, Herman articulated how these psychological responses are not merely symptoms but are deeply intertwined with the individual's attempt to cope with unrelenting trauma. This insight laid the groundwork for understanding how trauma affects not just the mind but also the body, influencing emotional regulation, memory, and behavior.

While the symptoms of C-PTSD share similarities with those of Post-Traumatic Stress Disorder (PTSD) as outlined in the DSM-5, they also encompass additional dimensions. Beyond experiencing flashbacks, avoiding reminders, and feeling constantly on edge, individuals with C-PTSD often struggle with affect dysregulation, a negative self-concept, and disrupted relationships. These symptoms reflect the complex and multifaceted nature of trauma's effects on mental health and interpersonal functioning.

Central to understanding C-PTSD is the interplay between early childhood trauma and attachment. Herman's work illuminated how traumatic experiences during formative years profoundly shape individuals' emotional regulation, self-perception, and ability to form and maintain healthy relationships. These early traumas disrupt the development of secure attachment bonds, leading to significant difficulties in trusting others and feeling safe in intimate connections.

Herman's insights also anticipated the physiological changes that trauma can induce in the brain, long before these were fully understood in the field of neuroscience. She highlighted how trauma could alter neural pathways and affect the brain's stress response system, contributing to heightened arousal, hypervigilance, and emotional dysregulation. These physiological changes further exacerbate the psychological and interpersonal challenges faced by individuals with C-PTSD, making Herman's early recognition of these patterns even more remarkable.

Recognizing and addressing the multifaceted nature of C-PTSD is crucial for clinicians working with survivors of childhood trauma. Herman's work encourages a comprehensive approach that addresses not only the immediate symptoms but also the broader psychological and interpersonal repercussions of trauma. This may involve integrating trauma-informed therapies, such as trauma-focused cognitive behavioral therapy and dialectical behavior therapy, to help individuals regulate their emotions, challenge negative beliefs about themselves, and cultivate healthier relationship patterns.

Judith Herman's pioneering work on C-PTSD has transformed our understanding of trauma and its lasting impact on survivors. By recognizing the complex interplay between early childhood trauma, attachment, and the subsequent physiological changes in the brain, Herman paved the way for more effective and compassionate approaches to supporting survivors of childhood trauma. Her insights continue to guide clinicians in providing trauma-informed care that empowers survivors on their journey toward healing and recovery.

Chapter 5

THE ROLE OF THE THERAPEUTIC RELATIONSHIP IN HEALING TRAUMA AND ATTACHMENT WOUNDS

Attachment theory offers a framework for understanding how early relationships with primary caregivers shape an individual's emotional and relational experiences throughout life. It interweaves genetics, temperament (often categorized by the Big Five Personality traits), and the interaction between the child and their caregiver, typically the mother. Attachment patterns, formed during childhood, have lasting effects on how individuals perceive and engage in relationships as adults. These patterns often translate into how clients approach their therapeutic and adult relationships, revealing much about their broader relational dynamics.

There are three primary categories of attachment: secure, anxious, and avoidant. These categories provide insight into the foundational ways individuals seek connection and security, or, conversely, how they distance themselves from vulnerability and emotional reliance on others.

A secure attachment forms when a caregiver encourages the child to explore the world and returns with curiosity and validation. In this scenario, the caregiver creates a safe base from which the child can confidently venture out, knowing they have a secure and supportive place to return. The child's exploration is met with curiosity about their experiences and world view, reinforcing a sense of trust in relationships and emotional safety.

In contrast, an anxious attachment develops when a caregiver instills fear about the world, encouraging the child to stay close for security. The child learns that safety lies in proximity to the caregiver, which translates into an adult experience of clinginess or fear of abandonment in relationships. The individual may constantly seek reassurance and validation from others, doubting their ability to manage distress on their own.

An avoidant attachment is formed when a child is encouraged to explore but, upon returning to the caregiver, is met with disinterest or a lack of support. If the child is dysregulated or distressed, the caregiver might encourage them to resolve their emotions on their own, often leaving the child feeling isolated and unsupported. As adults, those with avoidant attachments tend to distance themselves emotionally, preferring independence over vulnerability. They may avoid intimacy and have difficulty relying on others for emotional support, often retreating into self-reliance to manage their internal world.

Typically, individuals experience a combination of these attachment narratives, but understanding a client's default attachment style offers significant insight into how they will engage with the therapeutic relationship and how they navigate relationships in their adult lives.

For example, a client with an anxious attachment may be overly reliant on the therapist for reassurance, constantly seeking validation and support, while someone with an avoidant attachment might struggle to open up or trust the therapeutic process, keeping emotional distance even in moments of vulnerability. A securely attached individual will likely engage more readily, using the therapeutic relationship as a space for exploration and growth, trusting in the process of healing.

The therapeutic relationship offers a powerful pathway for healing trauma and repairing disrupted attachments, particularly when clients have used external relationships or behaviors—what we often refer to as "shiny objects"—to avoid confronting deeper emotional wounds. Trauma can severely disrupt a person's ability to form healthy attachments, often leading to relational patterns that replicate their early attachment experiences. For instance, trauma survivors might repeat avoidance, anxiety, or a combination of both in adult relationships, mirroring the dynamics they experienced as children with their caregivers.

The therapeutic or sacred spaces allow these attachment wounds to be safely revisited and explored. The therapist, acting as a secure base, can model a healthy, attuned relationship, providing the client with experiences that may have been lacking in their early development. Through this relationship, clients can begin to challenge their ingrained attachment patterns and explore new, healthier ways of connecting with others.

For many men, societal expectations around masculinity further complicate these attachment issues. Men are often discouraged from expressing vulnerability or seeking emotional support, reinforcing avoidant or anxious attachment behaviors. This adds another layer to the complexity of healing from trauma, as men may be more prone to using distractions or performative behaviors (the shiny object) to cope with emotional pain, rather than addressing the underlying issues.

Therapy, however, provides an opportunity to disrupt these patterns. By integrating trauma theory with attachment theory, therapists can create a comprehensive understanding of how trauma impacts emotional and relational experiences. This is particularly valuable for male clients, who may struggle to see the connection between their past trauma and their current relationship difficulties. The therapeutic relationship becomes a safe and supportive environment where these dynamics can be explored, and where healing can begin to take place.

For instance, a male client who experienced an avoidant attachment with his mother might struggle with emotional intimacy in his adult relationships, distancing himself from his partner whenever vulnerability arises. In therapy, this dynamic can be gently unpacked. The therapist's consistent presence, attunement, and curiosity provide a corrective emotional experience, allowing the client to see that vulnerability does not necessarily lead to abandonment or rejection.

For individuals who have experienced interpersonal trauma, the impact of betrayal or divided loyalties can deeply disrupt their attachment model and affect their ability to engage in healthy relationships. Interpersonal trauma often involves someone close, someone trusted—a family member, partner, or friend—leading to a profound sense of betrayal. This betrayal does more than damage trust; it can reinforce or even exaggerate an individual's existing attachment style. For those with an anxious attachment, who already fear abandonment and crave closeness, the betrayal can make them hypervigilant in relationships. They may constantly be on the lookout for signs of disloyalty, obsessively scanning their partner's actions, tone, or behavior for any indication that they are about to be abandoned. This hyperawareness becomes a defense mechanism, a way to stay one step ahead of the anticipated rejection. In this anxious state, they may become clingy or controlling, attempting to preempt betrayal by staying emotionally over-involved, which can paradoxically push partners away.

On the other hand, individuals with an avoidant attachment style, which is often more prevalent in males, may react to trauma and betrayal by justifying emotional distancing. For them, the betrayal is a confirmation of their belief that emotional closeness is unsafe, and vulnerability leads to pain. This attachment style often leads them to suppress their emotions, avoid intimate connections, and maintain a sense of emotional detachment from their partners. In the wake of trauma, these avoidant individuals might increase their emotional distance, using the betrayal as further evidence that keeping people at arm's length is the safest strategy. They may even use the betrayal as a rationalization for not engaging emotionally in relationships, further reinforcing their internal belief that vulnerability is a weakness.

The impact of betrayal in interpersonal trauma also introduces the complex dynamic of divided loyalties, which can further distort an individual's ability to form healthy attachments. For example, in cases of familial abuse, the survivor may feel torn between loyalty to the family member who betrayed them and the instinct to protect themselves. This internal conflict can create a psychological split, where the survivor struggles to reconcile love, loyalty, and betrayal, complicating their relationships with others. In some cases, the survivor may feel obligated to maintain ties with their abuser, either out of fear, societal pressure, or a sense of duty, which only deepens their attachment struggles.

When these attachment wounds are left unhealed, the individual may experience a repeated pattern of emotional disconnection in their adult relationships. They might avoid intimacy altogether or engage in superficial connections, all the while remaining hypervigilant to any signs of potential betrayal. For avoidant individuals, this pattern can become a self-fulfilling prophecy. By withdrawing emotionally and failing to invest in relationships, they reinforce the cycle of isolation, further distancing themselves from the possibility of healthy attachment and healing. Their sense of emotional invulnerability becomes a shield, but one that keeps them disconnected and lonely.

In both anxious and avoidant attachment styles, the role of betrayal becomes an ingrained narrative that further entrenches dysfunctional relational patterns. Survivors of interpersonal trauma find it difficult to trust themselves and others, often believing that they are either unworthy of genuine connection or destined to be betrayed again. This emotional landscape becomes fraught with fear, distrust, and avoidance, preventing them from engaging fully in relationships or accessing the emotional healing they need.

The challenge in therapy is to help these individuals recognize the ways in which trauma has shaped their attachment patterns and how those patterns are affecting their current relationships. For the anxiously attached, this means working to reduce hypervigilance and develop a sense of safety and security that does not rely on constant reassurance from their partner. For the avoidantly attached, the therapeutic process involves gently challenging their belief that emotional distancing protects them from harm and encouraging them to gradually open up to vulnerability and emotional connection.

The therapist's role is crucial in navigating this delicate terrain. By creating a secure, non-judgmental therapeutic environment, the therapist can model a healthier attachment, offering the client a safe space to explore their fears, needs, and vulnerabilities. Through this process, the client can begin to untangle the deeply rooted patterns of betrayal and abandonment, learning to trust again and rebuild the capacity for healthy, secure relationships. By focusing on the underlying attachment issues that stem from betrayal, therapy can become a powerful space for individuals to rewrite their relational narratives, moving away from fear and avoidance toward a place of trust, connection, and healing.

The goal of therapy, in this context, is not just to understand the attachment style but to transform it. The therapeutic relationship serves as a bridge between the client's past and present, offering a new model for relationships where trust, emotional safety, and connection are possible. This process, while gradual, enables clients to begin to form healthier attachments in their personal lives, breaking free from the patterns of avoidance, anxiety, or compulsive repetition that once defined their relationships.

In summary, attachment theory provides a crucial framework for understanding how early relationships shape adult relational patterns, particularly in the context of trauma. For male survivors of sexual abuse, the intersection of trauma, gender expectations, and attachment theory highlights the complex interplay between emotional needs, societal pressures, and personal identity. By fostering a secure, attuned therapeutic relationship, therapists can help clients navigate these challenges, ultimately empowering them to build healthier, more fulfilling relationships in their lives.

HEALING THROUGH THE THERAPEUTIC RELATIONSHIP: A CASE EXAMPLE

In the context of John's journey, the therapeutic relationship became a vital foundation for moving beyond judgment and into a space of curiosity and understanding. When John first came into therapy, his behaviors—soliciting sex workers—were seen through the lens of shame and deviance, both by himself and by those around him. These behaviors served as his "shiny object," a distraction that kept him from confronting the deeper wounds of his past. His external relationships with these women were not merely acts of infidelity; they were rooted in an attempt to reclaim a sense of control that had been brutally taken from him during his childhood trauma.

In therapy, trust was the cornerstone that allowed John to begin this difficult work. The therapeutic relationship provided a secure, non-judgmental space where John could explore his behaviors without fear of condemnation. This trust was essential because it allowed John to shift from a place of self-judgment to one of curiosity—an openness to understanding why he was engaging in these destructive patterns.

As we delved into his past, John started to see the connections between his current actions and his early experiences of sexual trauma. His compulsion to seek out similar sexual experiences, with the roles now reversed, was not about deviance but a desperate attempt to regain control in situations where he felt powerless. The therapeutic relationship offered John the safety he needed to explore these painful memories and recognize how they were still influencing his life.

This process of exploration was not just about uncovering the roots of his behaviors but also about empowering John to see that these actions had a function—they were attempts to manage overwhelming feelings of chaos and helplessness. Understanding this allowed John to reframe his behaviors, not as mere failures or moral lapses, but as misguided strategies to cope with unresolved trauma.

Through the therapeutic relationship, John was able to take a "leap of faith" away from his reliance on these external distractions and towards deeper, more meaningful healing. The trust he developed in therapy gave him the courage to face his trauma head-on and to explore new ways of achieving control in his life that did not involve self-destructive behaviors. This shift from judgment to curiosity, facilitated by the safety of the therapeutic relationship, marked a crucial turning point in John's journey toward recovery.

ATTACHMENT THEORY AND THE POWER OF THE THERAPEUTIC RELATIONSHIP

Attachment theory suggests that early interactions with primary caregivers significantly influence an individual's lifelong patterns of relating to others. When these early relationships are disrupted—whether through neglect, inconsistency, or emotional unavailability—it can create vulnerabilities that make individuals more susceptible to further trauma, including interpersonal sexual abuse. In this context, the "shiny object" is the way these early attachment disruptions set the stage for future relational dynamics where an offender might exploit these vulnerabilities. The violation of attachment doesn't necessarily stem solely from the trauma of abuse itself but can also originate from the fractured relationship with primary caregivers.

For men who have experienced trauma, these early disruptions in attachment can lead to profound challenges in forming and maintaining healthy adult relationships. Societal expectations that equate masculinity with emotional stoicism further compound these difficulties, making it harder for them to connect deeply with others and to seek help when they need it.

This is where the therapeutic relationship becomes paramount in the healing process. The consistent, empathetic, and reliable environment provided by the therapist offers a new relational experience—one that can help repair the broken attachment patterns established in early life. This therapeutic relationship serves as a corrective emotional experience, allowing clients to rebuild the trust and safety that may have been compromised not just by the trauma of abuse but by the foundational disruptions in their primary relationships.

Through this relationship, clients can explore how their past experiences have shaped their attachment patterns and begin to develop healthier ways of relating to themselves and others. The therapeutic process allows individuals to work through the emotional and cognitive distortions that trauma and early attachment disruptions have created, offering a path to healing that is deeply rooted in relational safety.

A critical aspect of this journey is the therapist's role as a "fair witness." This concept involves creating the necessary boundaries and support to provide a secure base from which clients can explore their vulnerabilities. The therapist, acting as a fair witness, helps clients navigate and correct the emotional and cognitive distortions that have taken root, while also fostering the courage to trust others again.

In this role, the therapist offers a balanced perspective, challenging clients' distorted beliefs and helping them reframe their experiences. This non-judgmental and supportive environment is essential for clients to explore difficult emotions and memories, knowing that they are held with compassion and understanding. As clients begin to heal these internal wounds, they gain the confidence to extend trust beyond the therapeutic relationship, laying the groundwork for healthier relationships in their lives.

By establishing this secure base, therapists empower clients to take the necessary steps toward healing, both within themselves and in their relationships with others. This transformative process is supported by the therapist's role as a fair witness.

UNRAVELLING SELF-SABOTAGE AND THE PARALLEL PROCESS IN THERAPY

Self-sabotage is a common yet often overlooked narrative that can significantly impact trust within relationships, particularly for individuals who have experienced interpersonal trauma. In the therapeutic setting, it is crucial to recognize and address patterns of self-sabotage, as they often function as protective mechanisms. These mechanisms create barriers to intimacy and trust, effectively shielding clients from potential emotional harm. However, while these behaviors may offer short-term protection, they ultimately hinder the development of healthy, trusting relationships.

Within the therapeutic relationship, identifying potential ruptures—moments when clients feel particularly vulnerable or perceive a threat to their emotional safety—is essential. These are the moments when self-sabotage is most likely to surface, as the client's instinct to protect themselves kicks in. By proactively addressing these patterns, therapists can create a secure and supportive environment where clients feel safe to explore their fears and vulnerabilities. This understanding of self-sabotage as a form of self-preservation allows clients to recognize these behaviors in themselves and work toward developing healthier coping strategies.

The concept of the parallel process further deepens our understanding of these dynamics. The parallel process suggests that the interactions and emotional dynamics within the therapeutic relationship often reflect the client's external relationships. Originally identified by Harold Seales and later expanded upon by others, this concept emphasizes the interconnectedness of the therapeutic and personal experiences.

In therapy, recognizing the parallel process can provide valuable insights into the client's behavior and attachment patterns. For instance, the ways in which a client might sabotage the therapeutic relationship—perhaps by pushing boundaries, withholding trust, or retreating emotionally—can mirror how they behave in other significant relationships. By reflecting on these parallels, clients can develop greater self-awareness, understanding how their internal processes and defense mechanisms play out in various aspects of their lives.

Integrating the recognition of self-sabotage with an understanding of the parallel process offers a powerful approach to therapy. It allows clients to not only identify and address self-sabotaging behaviors but also to see how these patterns are replicated in their broader relational world. Through this combined lens, clients can begin to break the cycle of self-sabotage, fostering healthier, more fulfilling connections both within and outside the therapeutic space.

In conclusion, the integration of attachment theory, trauma, and the therapeutic relationship offers a powerful framework for understanding and healing the complex emotional wounds experienced by male survivors of interpersonal sexual trauma. Early attachment disruptions and the impact of trauma can shape an individual's relational patterns well into adulthood, often leading to dysfunctional behaviors and self-sabotage. However, through the creation of a secure, attuned, and supportive therapeutic environment, therapists can provide a corrective emotional experience that fosters healing. By addressing the deep-seated issues of attachment, trust, and vulnerability, therapy offers clients the opportunity to break free from the cycles of avoidance, anxiety, and emotional disconnection. Ultimately, this process allows for the development of healthier, more fulfilling relationships and the possibility of true emotional recovery.

Chapter 6

CHALLENGING MASCULINE NORMS: HOW TRADITIONAL GENDER EXPECTATIONS SHAPE TRAUMA RESPONSES

Gender is increasingly understood as a spectrum rather than a binary concept. This perspective embraces diverse identities and acknowledges the complexity of individual experiences. Gender theory delves into the ways societal norms and expectations shape not only how masculinity and femininity are defined but also how they are performed in daily life. These dynamics—including social constructs, intersectionality, power relations, and the impact of toxic masculinity—play a significant role in shaping the experiences of male survivors of sexual abuse.

Gender is not merely a biological reality but a social construct, heavily influenced by cultural norms. For male survivors of sexual trauma, these societal expectations can profoundly affect how they perceive and cope with their experiences. Traditional ideas of masculinity often discourage vulnerability and seeking help, pushing men toward emotional withdrawal, avoidance, and anxiety. This creates a significant barrier to recovery, as these men struggle to reconcile their traumatic experiences with the rigid expectations placed on them.

The shiny object in this context is the societal narrative that equates masculinity with emotional stoicism and control. This narrative not only dictates how men are expected to behave but also how they internalize their trauma. For instance, the pressure to "toughen up" can lead men to suppress their emotions, viewing vulnerability as a weakness. This often results in men taking pride in their ability to emotionally distance themselves from their trauma. While this may seem protective in the short term, it ultimately hinders genuine healing by preventing men from processing their trauma and developing healthier coping mechanisms.

Furthermore, the intersection of gender with other aspects of identity—such as race, sexuality, and socioeconomic status—adds complexity to how male survivors experience trauma. Cultural expectations around masculinity can vary, influencing how men seek support or express emotions. These expectations often lead to emotional withdrawal, making it difficult for men to engage fully in recovery, as they internalize the belief that showing emotion is a sign of weakness.

In therapy, the influence of these gender norms becomes evident. Male survivors may find it challenging to establish trust or engage authentically due to the internalized pressure to maintain a façade of strength. Therapists, too, can be influenced by these norms, sometimes reinforcing harmful narratives by avoiding discussions that would require male clients to confront their vulnerabilities. This dynamic can perpetuate feelings of shame and guilt, making it even more difficult for male survivors to heal.

Understanding the impact of gender norms is crucial for developing effective therapeutic approaches. The role of the therapist is not just to address the symptoms of trauma but to challenge the societal expectations that hinder recovery. By fostering an environment where emotional expression and vulnerability are encouraged and seen as strengths, therapists can help male clients move beyond the distractions of these societal "shiny objects" and focus on the deeper work of healing.

Gender theory also highlights how these societal norms impact relationships. Men who adhere to the "toughen up" narrative often struggle to form deep, intimate connections. Their relationships may remain superficial, as they avoid emotional closeness to protect themselves from perceived vulnerability. This avoidance can lead to a cycle of isolation and disconnection, further complicating their recovery process.

Moreover, the influence of the therapist's gender on the therapeutic process cannot be overlooked. Male therapists, shaped by the same societal expectations, may unconsciously avoid sensitive discussions, reinforcing the very norms that their clients need to challenge. This avoidance can stifle the therapeutic process, preventing male clients from fully engaging in the work necessary for healing.

To break this cycle, it is essential to create a therapeutic environment where men feel safe to explore their emotions without fear of judgment. Therapists must be aware of their own biases and the ways in which gender norms influence their interactions with clients. By actively challenging these expectations and supporting men in developing healthier coping mechanisms, therapists can help clients build stronger, more meaningful connections in their lives.

Ultimately, the integration of gender theory into the therapeutic process is vital for supporting male survivors of sexual trauma. Recognizing how societal norms shape avoidance, anxiety, and repetition allows therapists to tailor their interventions to address the unique challenges faced by male clients. By fostering a therapeutic environment that values authenticity and vulnerability, therapists can help men take the necessary steps toward healing, breaking free from the constraints of traditional masculinity, and forming deeper, more fulfilling relationships.

Chapter 7

SEXUAL DEVELOPMENT AND TRAUMA: THE INTERSECTION OF IDENTITY AND BEHAVIOR

Sexual development is a complex and multifaceted process that intertwines with various aspects of a person's life, from their physical sensations to their identity and relational experiences. Dennis Dailey's Circle of Sexuality highlights five fundamental components of sexual development: Sensuality, Intimacy, Sexual Identity, Sexual Health, and Sexualization. For male survivors of sexual trauma, understanding these components through the lens of trauma provides critical insight into how their sexual behaviors and perceptions are shaped by their past. The "shiny object" in this exploration often lies in the behaviors or coping mechanisms that manifest as a distraction from deeper issues rooted in trauma. These behaviors may serve an adaptive function in the short term but often become problematic when they fail to address the underlying causes of distress.

SENSUALITY AND DISCONNECTION

Sensuality refers to an individual's capacity to experience physical sensations and derive pleasure from their body. Trauma can profoundly disrupt this connection. For many male survivors of interpersonal sexual trauma, the body becomes a site of discomfort or even shame. They may experience dissociation from their physical sensations, finding it difficult to fully engage with or enjoy touch. This disconnect can manifest in behaviors where the individual either avoids physical intimacy altogether or engages in it compulsively, using the act itself as a distraction from the deeper discomfort they feel within their bodies. This "shiny object" of compulsive sexual behavior is not about pleasure but about numbing or escaping from the lingering pain of trauma. The avoidance or overindulgence in sensual experiences often reflects a distorted relationship with the body, which requires careful exploration in therapy to begin reconnecting with the body in a healthy, non-traumatic way.

INTIMACY AND TRUST

Intimacy, the ability to form close and trusting relationships, often becomes particularly challenging for trauma survivors, especially male survivors of sexual trauma. Attachment style and gender expectations play significant roles in how men navigate intimacy and vulnerability. For many men, societal norms have long discouraged emotional openness and vulnerability, positioning them as traits that contradict traditional notions of masculinity. These gendered expectations create an environment where male survivors may struggle to reconcile their need for connection with the fear of judgment or rejection.

Male survivors who have experienced relational trauma often carry deep attachment wounds. An anxious attachment style may cause men to constantly seek approval or validation, fearing abandonment, yet simultaneously pushing intimacy away due to the fear of being hurt. For avoidant men, who may have learned early on that vulnerability leads to pain, intimacy is controlled and distanced, often manifesting as a pattern of serial relationships or encounters devoid of emotional connection. This avoidant attachment style aligns with societal messages that discourage men from expressing their emotional needs, reinforcing the idea that they must handle their pain alone.

In this dynamic, the "shiny object" becomes sexual encounters that are free from emotional vulnerability or any deeper relational connection. These interactions are safer because they do not require the man to expose his inner self or face the potential for rejection. Men with avoidant attachment styles may gravitate toward physical intimacy as a way to experience closeness without risking the emotional depth that might make them feel vulnerable. However, this coping mechanism perpetuates a cycle of emotional isolation, keeping them at a distance from real intimacy, which could foster genuine healing.

For men with anxious attachment styles, the fear of betrayal or rejection can create an overwhelming need to control relationships. They may crave intimacy, yet push it away when it becomes too close, fearing that their partner will abandon them once they truly see who they are. This creates a push-pull dynamic in which intimacy is sought, yet kept at arm's length. The fear of judgment—both from others and from themselves—keeps them in a constant state of emotional turmoil, never fully able to trust or connect with others.

Therapy, particularly in a group setting, offers an opportunity to explore these intersectional dynamics of attachment, trauma, and gender. In a non-judgmental, confidential space, men can begin to challenge the societal messages that tell them vulnerability is a weakness. They can also explore how their attachment styles influence their relationships and how their avoidance or anxious behaviors have prevented them from forming deeper, more meaningful connections.

By fostering curiosity about their attachment patterns and exploring the deeper fears driving their behavior, men can begin to rewrite their narratives around intimacy. They can learn that emotional closeness does not have to be feared, and that vulnerability can be a source of strength rather than weakness. The shiny objects of avoidance, physical encounters, or surface-level connections lose their allure as men start to recognize that true intimacy offers a path to healing and self-acceptance.

As they begin to form healthier attachment bonds within the therapeutic environment, men can carry these new insights into their personal relationships. Over time, the need to keep intimacy controlled or at a distance diminishes, and the possibility of deeper, more fulfilling connections becomes attainable. By recognizing the intersectionality of attachment, trauma, and gender, therapy provides men with the tools to move beyond their past and toward a future where intimacy is no longer feared, but embraced as a key component of healing.

SEXUAL IDENTITY AND SHAME

Sexual identity, encompassing one's understanding and acceptance of their sexual orientation or gender identity, can be profoundly affected by trauma. Trauma disrupts the natural development of sexual identity, often leading to confusion, shame, and internalized beliefs that something is inherently flawed or defective within oneself. This confusion becomes even more complicated when sexual trauma is involved, as the survivor may struggle to untangle the pleasure they experienced during the abuse from their sexual identity. The reality that many of the sexual encounters were physically pleasurable adds a layer of complexity to the trauma, creating a painful intersection between the physical sensations of pleasure and the deep psychological scars left by the abuse. This can lead to significant confusion, as the survivor may equate their sexual identity with the trauma, perpetuating feelings of shame and a sense of defectiveness.

For many men, especially those in the LGBTQ community, these experiences are compounded by societal pressures and stigma surrounding masculinity and sexual orientation. Some men may begin to question their sexual identity because of the trauma, leading to confusion about whether their attraction to the same sex is an authentic part of who they are or merely a result of the abuse. This confusion can perpetuate shame, making it difficult for survivors to reconcile their physical desires with their sense of self. For some, this may lead them to identify as gay, while others may engage in sexual encounters with men but resist identifying as gay, adding further complexity to their understanding of their sexual identity.

In many cases, the sexual identity of these men becomes intertwined with the trauma itself, leaving them unsure of whether their sexual behavior is a reflection of their true self or a compulsive repetition of their abuse. Untangling these variables is crucial for the survivor's healing process. By exploring the origins of these feelings and behaviors, therapists can help clients discern the difference between what is rooted in compulsive repetition—a survival mechanism often seen in trauma survivors—and what is part of their authentic sexual identity. Helping men understand these distinctions allows them to begin separating their trauma from their identity, fostering greater clarity and self-acceptance.

Another critical variable to consider in untangling sexual identity from trauma is the romantic component of relationships. Sexual encounters, while often the focus of confusion, are just one piece of the puzzle. Exploring a client's romantic feelings—how they experience emotional intimacy, connection, and love—can provide additional insight into their authentic self. By helping clients reflect on not just their sexual experiences but their romantic desires and attachments, therapists can support them in gaining a fuller understanding of their identity beyond the confines of trauma-driven behaviors.

Hypermasculinity regarding gender, often arises as a response to trauma for male survivors of sexual abuse, serving as a defense mechanism to cope with both the abuse itself and societal expectations around masculinity. In many cultures, particularly in American society, there is a deeply ingrained belief that men should be strong, invulnerable, and dominant. These gender norms leave little room for vulnerability or victimhood, particularly for men who have experienced sexual abuse. The need to assert hypermasculinity can serve two primary functions for these men: first, to prevent future victimization by projecting an image of strength and invulnerability, and second, to reclaim their sense of masculinity, which may feel threatened by their traumatic experiences.

For male survivors, the experience of sexual abuse is often intertwined with their sense of gender identity, especially in a society that tells men they cannot be victims. The trope that "real men" are tough, assertive, and emotionally restrained runs counter to the realities faced by men who have experienced victimization. In this cultural context, admitting to being sexually abused can feel like an admission of weakness, which goes against the hypermasculine ideal.

As a result, many male survivors adopt hypermasculine behaviors to distance themselves from the perception of victimhood and to reassert their masculinity.

One of the ways hypermasculinity manifests in survivors is through the adoption of traditionally masculine "shiny objects" such as guns, trucks, and sports, which serve as symbols of strength, control, and invulnerability. These objects become essential in the survivor's identity, as they are outward markers of their reclaimed masculinity. For many, this hypermasculine persona, bolstered by an attachment to these objects, acts as a protective shield. The belief is that if they can embody what society deems as masculine—projecting dominance and control through aggression, material symbols, or physical prowess—they will never again be vulnerable to the kind of exploitation they experienced in the past. This often translates into excessive physicality in sports, emotional detachment in relationships, or even hypersexuality, where sex becomes another arena to assert dominance rather than foster genuine connection. These behaviors, like the attachment to hypermasculine symbols, serve as coping mechanisms to avoid deeper emotional wounds and the fear of appearing weak or vulnerable.

The intersection of hypermasculinity and sexuality is particularly complex for male survivors of sexual trauma. In American culture, the stereotype that gay men are feminine or weak further complicates how survivors process their trauma, especially if their abuse involved same-sex encounters. For these men, engaging in hypermasculine behaviors may be a way to distance themselves from the internalized stigma associated with being a victim or the perceived femininity linked with same-sex attraction. By embracing hypermasculinity, they attempt to reclaim their gender identity, reinforcing their status as "real men," despite the shame or confusion they may feel about their sexual experiences.

In many cases, male survivors of sexual trauma may have experienced physical pleasure during the abuse, which can be deeply confusing and contribute to feelings of shame. Society often portrays sexual pleasure as something that should be enjoyed, yet when it occurs in the context of abuse, it becomes intertwined with trauma and guilt. For survivors, the fact that their bodies responded to the abuse in a way that felt pleasurable can lead to profound internal conflict about their masculinity and sexuality. They may question whether their physical responses mean that they wanted or enjoyed the abuse, which can reinforce feelings of defectiveness.

To cope with this confusion, some men lean into hypermasculine behaviors as a way of distancing themselves from these uncomfortable feelings. By embracing the idea that being a "real man" means being strong, dominant, and sexually aggressive, they try to overwrite the vulnerability they felt during their abuse. Hypersexuality, in particular, can become a way for these men to reclaim a sense of control over their bodies and their sexual experiences, even if it leads to emotional disconnection and unhealthy relationships.

This dynamic becomes even more complicated for men in the LGBTQ community. For some gay men, their abuse may have occurred in the context of same-sex relationships or encounters, which can blur the lines between trauma and sexual identity. In a society that often portrays gay men as feminine or weak, survivors may feel pressured to adopt hypermasculine behaviors to avoid being further stigmatized. Hypermasculinity, in this sense, becomes a tool for asserting their gender identity while simultaneously masking the shame or confusion they may feel about their sexual orientation.

For other men who do not identify as gay but have had sexual experiences with men, the trauma of abuse can further complicate their understanding of their sexual identity. Some survivors may engage in sexual behaviors with men but refuse to identify as gay, using hypermasculinity as a way to rationalize or distance themselves from the implications of their behavior. This allows them to maintain a sense of control over their identity, even if it means living in denial about the true nature of their desires.

Ultimately, hypermasculinity serves as a protective shield for male survivors of sexual trauma, allowing them to avoid confronting the deeper emotional wounds that their trauma has left behind. However, this defense mechanism can also prevent them from healing, as it reinforces the very gender norms and societal expectations that contribute to their shame and confusion in the first place. By focusing on dominance, control, and strength, male survivors may be avoiding the vulnerability that is necessary for real emotional connection and intimacy.

Therapy plays a critical role in helping these men untangle the complex relationship between their trauma, their gender identity, and their sexuality. By creating a safe, non-judgmental space, therapists can help survivors explore how their experiences have shaped their understanding of masculinity and sexuality. This process often involves challenging the societal messages that equate vulnerability with weakness and helping survivors recognize that they can still be masculine without having to adopt hypermasculine behaviors.

Moreover, therapists can help survivors understand that their sexual experiences—both during the abuse and in their adult lives— do not define their masculinity. By fostering curiosity rather than judgment, therapists can guide survivors in exploring the differences between compulsive repetition of trauma-driven behaviors and authentic expressions of their sexuality. This allows survivors to reclaim their sense of self, free from the distortions imposed by both the trauma and societal expectations around masculinity.

In the end, the goal is to help male survivors realize that their masculinity is not contingent on how dominant, aggressive, or unemotional they are. True masculinity, and true healing, come from embracing vulnerability, forming meaningful connections, and understanding that their worth as men is not diminished by the trauma they experienced. By dismantling the false narratives that hypermasculinity perpetuates, survivors can begin to redefine their masculinity in a way that aligns with their authentic selves.

As men begin to explore these aspects of their sexual identity in therapy, they can start to reframe their experiences in a way that feels empowering rather than shameful. The therapeutic process allows survivors to confront the shame and judgment they've internalized, both from society and from themselves. By understanding the societal expectations around masculinity and sexuality, survivors can begin to challenge the messages that have kept them feeling defective and start to embrace a more nuanced, compassionate view of themselves.

Ultimately, the goal is to help survivors reconnect with their sexual identity in a way that feels authentic and affirming. This process requires patience and a willingness to explore the layers of shame, confusion, and fear that have become entangled with their sexual development. As survivors untangle these variables, they gain greater clarity about who they are and what they want from their relationships—both sexual and romantic. In doing so, they can begin to move away from the compulsive repetition of their trauma and toward a more fulfilling, genuine expression of their identity.

Men who have experienced interpersonal trauma, particularly sexual abuse, often face significant challenges in managing their sexual health. Trauma can deeply affect both their physical well-being and their relationships, leading to patterns of avoidance in seeking medical care and addressing sexual health issues. This avoidance exacerbates existing health problems and creates a cycle of shame, mistrust, and further emotional distance. For many men, societal expectations around masculinity compound these issues, making it harder to admit vulnerability or seek help.

Studies show that men who have experienced sexual abuse are at a heightened risk for sexually transmitted infections (STIs) and other health complications. Men who were sexually abused are 150% more likely to contract HIV compared to those without a history of abuse. Additionally, they are significantly more likely to engage in condomless sex, which increases the risk of STIs and other adverse health outcomes. This behavior, often driven by dissociation and trauma, reflects an underlying sense of worthlessness and self-neglect, where maintaining sexual health becomes less of a priority than managing the emotional fallout of trauma.

Avoidance of sexual health care can also stem from the profound feelings of shame and mistrust that many survivors experience. For male survivors, particularly, the stigma surrounding sexual abuse makes it difficult to seek help. Many men avoid discussing their trauma or seeking care due to the societal belief that men should be strong, stoic, and unaffected by vulnerability. This avoidance of care is part of a larger coping mechanism, often manifesting as a "shiny object" — a focus on anything but the trauma itself. Instead of addressing the underlying issue, survivors may turn to compulsive behaviors, risky sexual encounters, or emotional detachment to escape the deeper emotional pain.

Sexual dysfunction is another prevalent issue among male survivors. Men who have been sexually abused are three times more likely to experience erectile dysfunction and twice as likely to suffer from premature ejaculation. Despite the significant prevalence of these issues, there remains a lack of targeted research and treatment options for male survivors. Much of the existing research has focused on aggression and high-risk behaviors rather than the nuances of sexual dysfunction and its relationship to trauma. This leaves many men without the support they need to address both the physical and emotional aspects of their sexual health.

One major reason for the lack of research and available treatment is the underreporting of sexual abuse by men. Gender norms often discourage men from disclosing their trauma, reinforcing the false belief that men cannot be victims of sexual abuse. The internalized shame and fear of judgment further push men into silence, preventing them from seeking help. This silence perpetuates the cycle of trauma and avoidance, leading to worsening health outcomes and deeper emotional scars.

In addition to sexual dysfunction and risky behaviors, some survivors may feel compelled to validate their sense of defectiveness through self-destructive actions, such as engaging in risky sexual encounters without protection. The mindset of "if you really knew me, you wouldn't care about me" drives these behaviors, where the individual seeks to confirm their belief that they are unworthy of love, care, or healthy relationships. The acquisition of an STI, in this context, may feel like a validation of this negative self-perception.

Improving sexual health outcomes for male survivors requires a trauma-informed approach to healthcare. By understanding the complex interplay between trauma, sexual health, and behavior, healthcare providers can offer more compassionate, effective care. This includes fostering an environment where survivors feel safe to discuss their experiences and seek help without judgment. Transparency, open communication, and a focus on both physical and emotional well-being are essential to building trust with male survivors.

Healthcare providers should prioritize creating trauma-informed, supportive spaces for men to seek help, encouraging open dialogue about sexual health, and reducing the stigma around male vulnerability. This shift in perspective is necessary for helping men reclaim their sexual health and well-being, ultimately fostering healthier, more fulfilling relationships.

Ultimately, addressing sexual health for male survivors of trauma goes beyond treating physical symptoms. It requires acknowledging and addressing the emotional and psychological wounds that often drive risky behaviors, avoidance, and dysfunction. By adopting a holistic approach that encompasses emotional intimacy, communication, and trust, survivors can begin to rebuild their relationships with themselves and others, moving toward a healthier and more integrated sense of well-being..

SEXUALIZATION AND REPETITION

Sexualization refers to the way individuals perceive and understand the sexual aspects of life, and this too can be significantly distorted by trauma. For some male survivors, sexualization becomes hyper-focused, with behaviors such as compulsive pornography use, sex addiction, or risky sexual behaviors emerging as attempts to normalize their sexual experiences. This compulsive repetition, a key element of PTSD, reflects a desire to regain control over their narrative. By repeatedly engaging in the same behaviors, survivors may unconsciously attempt to resolve the trauma by mastering the circumstances that initially felt so out of control.

This compulsion can be understood as a "shiny object" in the sense that it distracts from the deeper emotional pain. The behavior becomes the focus, while the underlying trauma remains unaddressed. This is where the therapist's role is crucial in helping the client understand that the behavior is not the problem, but a symptom of the larger issue. By exploring the function of these behaviors—whether they serve as avoidance, a way to reclaim power, or a method of managing overwhelming emotions—therapists can guide survivors toward healthier ways of engaging with their sexuality.

RECLAIMING SEXUAL IDENTITY POST-TRAUMA

Understanding the development of sexuality through the five elements—Sensuality, Intimacy, Sexual Identity, Sexual Health, and Sexualization—offers a comprehensive framework for helping clients make sense of their experiences. Sensuality involves reconnecting with bodily sensations, allowing survivors to reclaim a positive relationship with their physical selves. Intimacy focuses on rebuilding trust and emotional connection, which may have been disrupted by trauma. Sexual Identity helps clients explore and affirm their true sexual orientation or gender identity, untangling it from the confusion and shame that trauma may have introduced. Sexual Health addresses both physical and mental well-being, emphasizing the importance of self-care and understanding the impact of trauma on sexual functioning. Lastly, Sexualization explores how sexual behaviors may have been influenced by trauma, helping clients differentiate between behaviors driven by compulsion and those that reflect their authentic desires. By integrating these elements, clients can discern the ways interpersonal trauma has shaped their sexual life and begin to reclaim their identity and sense of self.

Chapter 8

TAILORING HEALING: ADAPTING THERAPEUTIC APPROACHES TO DIVERSE PERSONALITY STYLES

Understanding the impact of personality traits and temperament styles on healing from interpersonal trauma is essential for effective therapy, especially when considering the concept of the "shiny object." By integrating the OCEAN framework—a model from the Big Five Personality traits developed by Costa and McCrae, which includes Openness vs. Closed-Mindedness, Conscientiousness vs. Impulsivity, Extraversion vs. Introversion, Agreeableness vs. Antagonism, and Neuroticism vs. Emotional Stability—therapists can gain a deeper understanding of how these traits influence a person's response to trauma and their path to recovery. Combining this framework with an analysis of temperament helps reveal individual coping and healing patterns, enabling more personalized and effective therapeutic interventions.

Openness vs. Closed-Mindedness reflects a person's willingness to engage with new ideas and experiences versus a preference for familiarity and routine. For trauma survivors, high openness can encourage exploration of different therapeutic methods, fostering adaptability and resilience. However, this trait can also become a shiny object when the constant search for new experiences or treatments becomes a way to avoid the hard, consistent work required for deep healing. These individuals might be drawn to the novelty of new therapeutic approaches as a distraction, rather than fully engaging in one method long enough to see meaningful results. Conversely, those with a closed-minded temperament may rely heavily on past experiences, using this rigidity as a form of avoidance, which can limit their ability to form new connections or heal from past wounds. Therapists must help clients strike a balance between openness to new experiences and the discipline required to engage deeply with their healing process.

Conscientiousness vs. Impulsivity involves a person's level of organization, responsibility, and goal orientation versus a tendency to act spontaneously without considering the consequences. Individuals high in conscientiousness may approach therapy with a structured mindset, diligently following through on treatment plans. However, this very trait can serve as a shiny object when the focus on order and control becomes a way to avoid the chaotic emotions stirred by trauma. Instead of engaging with the emotional core of their experiences, these clients might concentrate on achieving specific therapeutic "milestones," treating their recovery like a checklist. On the other hand, individuals with a more impulsive nature might struggle to maintain consistency in their therapeutic work, allowing momentary distractions or urges to pull them away from the deeper work needed for healing. Therapists can assist clients by encouraging them to balance their need for control with the necessity of embracing emotional vulnerability while helping impulsive clients develop strategies to stay engaged and committed to their recovery process.

Extraversion vs. Introversion is characterized by sociability, enthusiasm, and a tendency to seek out external stimulation versus a preference for solitude and introspection. Extroverted trauma survivors may find social interactions provide a sense of connection and support, which is vital for recovery. However, extroversion can also become a shiny object when used to avoid introspection. These individuals might immerse themselves in social activities to escape their internal struggles, using their busy social lives as a shield against facing their trauma. While social support is important, it is crucial for therapists to help extroverted clients balance their outward focus with necessary inward reflection, encouraging them to confront their trauma rather than continuously seeking external distractions. Introverted clients, while often adept at self-reflection, may need encouragement to build social support systems and engage with others, as isolation can exacerbate feelings of loneliness and hinder recovery.

Agreeableness vs. Antagonism highlights the difference between cooperative, compassionate individuals who value harmonious relationships and those who are more competitive, critical, or resistant to social harmony. Highly agreeable individuals may prioritize others' needs over their own, sometimes to the detriment of their healing. This trait can become a shiny object when self-sacrifice or avoidance of conflict prevents these individuals from addressing their own pain or setting necessary boundaries. In this context, agreeableness may serve as a distraction from the difficult work of confronting and processing trauma. Conversely, individuals who lean towards antagonism may engage in oppositional behaviors as a way to assert control and protect themselves from perceived threats, which can also function as a form of avoidance. Therapists working with clients low in agreeableness need to be particularly patient and consistent, demonstrating reliability and empathy to build a trusting relationship while guiding highly agreeable clients to recognize the importance of self-care and assertiveness.

Neuroticism vs. Emotional Stability reflects a tendency to experience negative emotions intensely, such as anxiety, fear, or depression, versus a calm and resilient approach to stress and uncertainty. This trait is often heightened in trauma survivors, making them more susceptible to intense emotional responses and creating a constant state of hyperarousal—a core symptom of PTSD. The shiny object in this context is the overwhelming focus on managing these symptoms, which can overshadow the deeper work of addressing the trauma itself. Clients may become preoccupied with controlling their anxiety or other symptoms, using this as a way to avoid delving into the underlying trauma. Therapy for these individuals might involve techniques to stabilize their emotional state, such as mindfulness or relaxation exercises, while gradually helping them explore and process their traumatic experiences.

Optimism and pessimism, as extensions of emotional stability and neuroticism, play a significant role in shaping an individual's broader personality and behavior. Optimists, who generally exhibit emotional stability, tend to approach challenges with confidence, believing in positive outcomes, which can bolster traits like openness, agreeableness, and conscientiousness. Their belief in their own resilience enables them to take risks, seek new experiences, and foster stronger social connections. On the other hand, pessimists, more aligned with neuroticism, often anticipate negative outcomes, which can perpetuate avoidance behaviors, reduce their willingness to explore new ideas (openness), and diminish their ability to trust others (agreeableness). This mindset may also contribute to lower levels of conscientiousness, as a sense of futility or self-doubt can undermine motivation and perseverance. Thus, the lens through which individuals view the world—either optimistically or pessimistically—can deeply influence how they express other elements of the Big Five personality traits.

Temperament style plays a similarly crucial role in shaping how individuals perceive and respond to their environment, particularly in the context of relationships. For instance, a person with a closed-minded temperament might struggle to adapt to new therapeutic approaches or consider alternative perspectives on their trauma. This resistance can be a shiny object that keeps them locked in familiar, albeit dysfunctional, patterns. Therapy for these individuals may focus on gently challenging their rigidity, fostering an environment where they feel safe enough to explore new ideas and approaches without feeling threatened.

In contrast, those with an open-minded temperament might be more willing to experiment with different therapeutic modalities, which can be both a strength and a potential distraction if it prevents them from committing to a single path long enough to achieve meaningful progress. Helping these clients find a balance between openness to new experiences and the discipline required to engage deeply with their healing process is key.

Temperament also affects how individuals manage relational dynamics. For example, a person who is highly agreeable may have a temperament that leads them to fawn over others, using agreeableness as a shiny object to avoid conflict or difficult emotions. This pattern can make it challenging for them to establish healthy boundaries, particularly in relationships where their trauma has been triggered. Conversely, individuals who lean towards antagonism may engage in oppositional behaviors as a way to assert control and protect themselves from perceived threats, which can be another form of avoidance. These behaviors, while seemingly protective, ultimately prevent deeper emotional engagement and healing.

The intersection of gender norms and personality traits adds another layer to this complexity. Traditional masculinity often discourages emotional expression, which can lead men to use their personality traits, such as extraversion or conscientiousness, as shiny objects to avoid confronting their trauma. For instance, a man who is highly extraverted may focus on his social success as a way to mask his internal struggles, while a highly conscientious man may obsess over his work or responsibilities to avoid dealing with his emotions.

Understanding the interplay between personality traits, temperament styles, and gender norms allows therapists to recognize the shiny objects that distract from true healing. By addressing these distractions and focusing on the underlying trauma, therapists can help clients move toward a more integrated and authentic recovery. This approach not only supports the individual's healing process but also fosters the development of healthier, more fulfilling relationships

BUILDING RESILIENCE: A COGNITIVE BEHAVIORAL THERAPY FRAMEWORK FOR TRAUMA RECOVERY

Imagine you're at the grocery store. You've just finished paying for your groceries and are about to leave when, suddenly, someone grabs your shoulder. In that split second, your mind races through a range of possibilities. Is someone trying to harm you? Is it a mistake? Or maybe someone wants your attention? These thoughts flash through your mind, but the belief you land on—whether conscious or unconscious—will determine your reaction and how you interpret what happens next.

Let's break this down using the Cognitive Behavioral Therapy (CBT) framework, which follows the **ABC** model: **A**ctivating Event, **B**elief, and **C**onsequence, both behavioral and emotional. In this scenario, the activating event is the unexpected grab on your shoulder. Your belief about this event could be, "Someone wants my attention," leading to the consequence of curiosity. You might turn around calmly, only to see a store employee holding your wallet, which you'd unknowingly left at the checkout. Relieved, you thank them, take your wallet, and continue with your day. The encounter is resolved without much fuss, and the initial belief—that someone was just trying to help—is validated, leading to no lasting emotional impact.

Now, consider a different belief: "Someone is trying to hurt me." This belief triggers a surge of fear or anger, particularly for men who might instinctively lean towards anger as a protective response. The consequence of this belief is a defensive reaction—you shove the person away, ready to protect yourself. As the person falls, you see that it's just the store employee trying to return your wallet. However, your initial belief that you were under attack feels validated—after all, someone grabbed you, and you defended yourself. This belief is further reinforced when the police arrive and, seeing your agitated state, initially agree that something serious must have happened.

But then, the police start gathering more information. They find out that the person who grabbed you was simply trying to return your wallet, and suddenly, their perspective shifts. They begin to question your reaction, and perhaps, your state of mind. This new data challenges your belief, making you feel as if the system that was supposed to protect you is now questioning your actions. If the police officer carries a bias, perhaps thinking, "This guy overreacted," or even, "There must be something wrong with him," it only adds to your sense of alienation and mistrust.

Now, imagine another variation: your belief is still that you're being attacked, but instead of fighting, you choose to flee. You run out of the store, heart pounding, without looking back. Later, you realize your wallet is missing, and you conclude it was stolen during the encounter. This conclusion fits perfectly with your initial belief—someone was out to get you. You call the police and report a robbery. When the police arrive, they see how distressed and agitated you are, and they initially validate your experience. This initial validation feels comforting, as it aligns with your belief that you were in danger.

However, as the investigation continues, the police discover that the store employee was simply trying to return your wallet. When they present this new information, it challenges your narrative, leading to confusion and a sense of betrayal. You might feel that the police, who were supposed to be on your side, are now casting doubt on your story. If the officer suggests that your reaction was an overreaction, this might reinforce a deeper, more damaging belief that you cannot trust your instincts or that your perspective is inherently flawed. This can validate a more insidious narrative that it's better not to speak up or that enduring hardships quietly is the safer option—an unfortunate, but common, belief among male victims of trauma.

This scenario illustrates the power of the ABC model in CBT. The Activating Event (someone grabbing your shoulder), filtered through your Belief ("Someone wants to help me" vs. "Someone is attacking me"), leads to very different Consequences (curiosity and relief vs. fear, anger, or a flight response). When your initial belief is reinforced by what happens next—like the police initially validating your fear—it can further entrench that belief, even if later evidence suggests it was a distortion.

The role of biases in this process is critical, not just on your part, but also on the part of others, such as the police officer. If the officer, upon seeing your disheveled state, assumes you are overreacting or unstable, it might lead to further questioning of your account, which can feel like a personal attack. This interaction could easily trigger a defense mechanism, reinforcing your original belief that the world is a dangerous place where you must always be on guard.

In therapy, the therapist's role is to act as a "fair witness," much like the police officer, but with the goal of exploring these beliefs without judgment. The therapist helps you to question whether the belief that led to your reaction is the only possible interpretation of the event. They might ask, "Could there have been another reason someone grabbed your shoulder?" or "What evidence do you have that someone was trying to harm you?"

This process is essential in helping clients challenge distorted beliefs that stem from past trauma, especially interpersonal trauma where the individual's trust has been violated. If a client has a history of being hurt or betrayed, particularly by people they should have been able to trust, their beliefs about safety, trust, and the intentions of others may be skewed. The challenge for the therapist is to gently guide the client towards a place where they can entertain alternative explanations—where curiosity can replace fear, and understanding can replace suspicion.

However, this is not just an intellectual exercise. For clients, particularly male clients influenced by societal norms around masculinity, questioning these beliefs requires a leap of faith. It requires them to step outside the protective shell that their beliefs have created and trust that not every interaction is a potential threat. This leap is often where the most significant healing occurs, but it can only happen in a therapeutic environment that feels safe, supportive, and non-judgmental.

In essence, the therapist's job is to help the client navigate through their ingrained belief systems, much like the police officer might sift through the facts of an incident. The difference is that, in therapy, the goal is not just to determine what happened but to help the client see how their interpretations of events are shaped by past experiences, and how these interpretations might be keeping them stuck in a cycle of fear and avoidance.

By fostering this sense of curiosity and openness, therapists can guide clients toward breaking free from the cycle of distorted beliefs and reactions. The goal is to help them slow down and critically evaluate their perceptions, asking themselves whether their reactions are truly based on the current reality or if they are echoes of past trauma. This shift from automatic, fear-based responses to thoughtful, considered reactions is a crucial step in healing from interpersonal trauma and breaking free from the grip of the "shiny object" that keeps them trapped in a cycle of mistrust and hypervigilance.

In the end, this therapeutic process is about rebuilding trust—trust in others, trust in oneself, and trust in the possibility of a safer, more balanced world. It's about helping clients take that leap of faith, with the therapist as a steady, non-judgmental presence, guiding them towards a place where curiosity replaces fear, and understanding replaces suspicion.

REVISITING JOHN'S JOURNEY: THE SHINY OBJECT, PERSONALITY, AND CBT

John was a man who, on the surface, had it all: a successful career, a loving wife, and a wide social network. His extroverted agreeableness and charm made him a magnet in both business and personal circles, and his colleagues often admired his ability to connect with others so effortlessly. But beneath this polished exterior lay a complex and unresolved narrative, shaped by early trauma and reinforced by a set of rigid, no longer functional beliefs.

John's life began to unravel when his wife, Carole, discovered that he had been soliciting sex workers—again. This was not the first time; it was a pattern that had persisted for years, always surfacing when John felt overwhelmed or out of control. The act of seeking out these encounters served as his shiny object—a distraction that kept him from confronting the deeper emotional wounds that had haunted him since childhood.

Years earlier, John had been sexually abused by his stepfather, a traumatic experience that left him feeling powerless and ashamed. This trauma had instilled in him a need to regain control, a need that manifested in various ways throughout his life. In adulthood, this need for control drove him to compulsively seek out sexual encounters where he could assert dominance, flipping the power dynamics of his past abuse. Yet, despite his outward confidence, John was deeply disconnected from his emotions. What he perceived as emotional stability was, in reality, a form of dissociation—a way to protect himself from the pain he had never fully processed.

John's personality style played a significant role in how he navigated his trauma and relationships. His closed-minded stance, which he saw as decisiveness and strength, prevented him from considering alternative perspectives that could lead to healing. He was extroverted and agreeable, traits that allowed him to maintain a facade of social success, but these same traits also masked his deeper struggles. His charm and social adeptness became the shiny objects that distracted both himself and others from the underlying issues. Meanwhile, his perceived emotional stability was actually a dissociation from his feelings, a protective mechanism that kept him from fully engaging with his pain.

As we revisit John's narrative through the lens of the Cognitive Behavioral Therapy (CBT) framework, it becomes clear how his personality traits influenced his responses to life's challenges. In CBT, we often talk about the ABC model: Activating Event, Belief, and Consequence. This framework helps individuals understand how their thoughts (B) about an event (A) lead to emotional and behavioral consequences (C). For John, the activating event was often a situation that made him feel undermined or out of control—perhaps a challenging interaction at work or a disagreement with Carole.

Given his closed-minded stance, John would interpret these events through a rigid belief system: "I need to regain control, or else I will be overpowered." This belief was deeply rooted in his unresolved trauma, and it led to predictable consequences—his compulsive behavior of seeking out sex workers as a way to reassert dominance and control. This behavioral consequence was not just a random act of self-sabotage; it was a calculated response to a belief that had been formed in the aftermath of his childhood trauma.

John's extroversion and agreeableness also played into this pattern. His social charm made it easy for him to find external distractions, such as these illicit encounters, while his agreeableness allowed him to justify his actions as necessary to maintain control in his life. Yet, this charm and agreeableness also made it difficult for him to face the reality of his situation. The consequences of his actions—strained relationships, a growing sense of shame, and the risk of losing his marriage—were things he would rather avoid acknowledging. His dissociation from his emotions further compounded the problem, as it allowed him to continue these behaviors without fully confronting the guilt and pain they caused.

In therapy, as we applied the ABC model to John's behaviors, it became clear that his rigid belief system was a significant barrier to change. His closed-mindedness made it difficult for him to entertain the idea that his actions were not merely reactions to external stressors but were also driven by unresolved internal conflicts. The challenge in therapy was to help John recognize that what he perceived as emotional stability was, in fact, an avoidance of his true feelings. This required him to take a leap of faith, to trust that exploring these uncomfortable emotions would not destabilize him but rather lead to deeper healing.

However, this process was complicated by John's previous experiences with challenges to his authority in the business world. When John made decisions that were later questioned or criticized by colleagues or business partners, his initial reaction was often defensive. His extroverted agreeableness, which had served him well in creating alliances and securing deals, would quickly give way to a more closed-off stance when his decisions were challenged. This defensiveness was rooted in the same need for control that drove his other behaviors. When his decisions were questioned, it felt like an assault on his competence and authority, triggering the belief that he needed to reassert control to maintain his status.

In these business contexts, John's defensive reactions were often validated by the initial responses of others. Colleagues might see his emotional reaction as a sign of his passion and commitment, reinforcing his belief that he was justified in defending his position. However, as more data came to light or as the situation evolved, these same colleagues might begin to question his decisions more critically, challenging his worldview. This shift often led John to feel further entrenched in his original stance, unwilling to consider new information or alternative perspectives. This dynamic mirrored the therapeutic process, where John's initial resistance to challenging his beliefs could be seen as a defense mechanism rooted in his past experiences.

The therapist's role here was crucial, serving as a fair witness who could observe and gently challenge John's perceptions without judgment. This therapeutic relationship offered John a space where he could safely explore his beliefs and begin to see that his need for control was rooted in past trauma, not present reality. The therapist provided alternative interpretations and encouraged John to question his automatic responses, helping him to see that his behaviors were not random but were driven by deeper fears and unresolved pain.

As John began to understand the function of his behaviors, he also started to see how his personality traits had both helped and hindered his progress. His extroverted agreeableness had allowed him to navigate social situations successfully, but it had also distracted him from addressing his internal struggles. His closed-mindedness, while giving him a sense of control, had kept him from exploring new ways of thinking that could lead to healing. And his perceived emotional stability had, in fact, been a form of dissociation, preventing him from fully engaging with his emotions.

Throughout this process, it was important to recognize the influence of gender norms on John's behavior. Society often discourages men from expressing vulnerability, equating emotional restraint with strength. For John, this meant that his dissociation from his feelings was not only a personal coping mechanism but also a reflection of societal expectations. His agreeable nature and extroversion allowed him to conform to these expectations, while his closed-mindedness kept him from questioning them. In therapy, we had to address these gendered expectations and help John see that true strength lay not in avoiding his emotions but in facing them head-on.

John's journey illustrates the complex interplay between personality traits, trauma responses, and societal norms. His story highlights the importance of understanding these traits not as fixed qualities but as factors that can influence both the challenges and the opportunities for growth in the healing process. By addressing the shiny objects that distracted him from his deeper issues—whether they were external distractions like his compulsive behaviors or internal ones like his rigid beliefs—John was able to begin the difficult but rewarding work of healing from his past and building a healthier future.

In the end, John learned to challenge his rigid beliefs and open himself up to new perspectives. He began to see that true control did not come from dominating others or avoiding his feelings but from understanding and integrating his emotions in a healthy way. This process required him to be curious about his own responses and to trust that exploring his vulnerabilities would ultimately lead to a stronger, more resilient self. The therapeutic relationship played a key role in this transformation, providing the safe space John needed to explore these issues and begin to change his life for the better.

As we continue to explore John's story and others like it, we can see how the CBT framework, combined with an understanding of personality styles and societal influences, offers a powerful tool for addressing the complex issues that arise from interpersonal trauma. By focusing on the underlying beliefs and how they drive behavior, therapy can help individuals break free from the cycles that keep them trapped in unhealthy patterns. Through this process, they can begin to reclaim control over their lives, not by avoiding their pain, but by facing it and learning to live with it in a healthier, more integrated way.

CULTIVATING HEALING ATTRIBUTES: 15 ESSENTIAL QUALITIES FOR DEEPENING AND RESTORING RELATIONSHIPS

Chapter 10

SELF-AWARENESS AND THE THERAPIST: THE JOURNEY TO "KNOW THYSELF"

In the therapeutic process with male survivors of sexual interpersonal trauma, the relationship between therapist and client is central to the journey of healing. This relationship, however, is not without its complexities, as it is influenced by various psychological and emotional dynamics that can either facilitate or hinder the client's recovery. Among these dynamics, the concept of countertransference plays a pivotal role. Countertransference refers to the therapist's emotional, cognitive, and behavioral responses to the client—responses that may be triggered by the client's narratives, behaviors, or even by the therapist's own unresolved issues. Understanding and managing countertransference is essential for providing effective and compassionate care to male survivors.

To help therapists navigate the complexities of countertransference and ensure that the therapeutic relationship remains a safe and supportive space for healing, there are specific characteristics that have been identified as crucial. These characteristics serve as vital guideposts, offering therapists the necessary framework to manage their own responses effectively while maintaining the focus on the client's healing journey.

In Section 2 of the book, these fifteen characteristics will be explored in depth. Each one offers insight into how therapists can recognize, understand, and manage countertransference, ensuring that it does not become an obstacle to the client's progress. By embracing these principles, therapists can create a therapeutic environment that is both compassionate and resilient, allowing male survivors to confront their trauma and move toward recovery with the support and understanding they need.

This exploration will delve into how these characteristics can be integrated into practice, providing therapists with practical strategies for maintaining the integrity of the therapeutic relationship. As we move forward, the focus will be on how these guiding principles can empower therapists to navigate the emotional landscape of therapy with greater awareness and effectiveness, ultimately fostering a more healing and transformative experience for their clients.

Countertransference can be likened to a "shiny object" in therapy—it captures attention, sometimes distracts from the primary focus, and requires careful management to avoid disrupting the therapeutic process. Just as a shiny object can allure and mesmerize, countertransference can subtly, yet powerfully, draw the therapist's focus away from the client's needs, leading to potential missteps in treatment. It is essential for therapists to recognize when they are being pulled in by this "shiny object" and to realign their focus on the client's healing journey.

At its core, countertransference is an interplay between the therapist's internal world and the client's external expressions. It emerges when the client's story or behavior triggers something within the therapist—perhaps a memory, an emotion, or a bias—that relates more to the therapist's own life than to the client's. This can lead to reactions that are less about the client and more about the therapist's personal history, unresolved conflicts, or unconscious beliefs. For male survivors, whose experiences of trauma are often compounded by societal expectations of masculinity, countertransference can manifest in ways that either reinforce harmful stereotypes or hinder the therapeutic process.

One of the most profound challenges in working with male survivors is navigating the societal constructs of masculinity that both therapist and client bring into the therapeutic space. These constructs often include notions of strength, stoicism, and self-reliance, which can create barriers to vulnerability and emotional expression. Therapists, whether consciously or unconsciously, may hold biases that align with these societal norms, leading them to expect or even encourage behaviors in their male clients that align with these ideals. For instance, a therapist might feel uncomfortable when a male client expresses deep vulnerability, which could trigger the therapist's own discomfort with vulnerability or challenge their beliefs about masculinity.

This is where the concept of "knowing thyself" becomes critical. Therapists must engage in ongoing self-reflection to understand their emotional responses, biases, and potential triggers. Self-awareness allows therapists to recognize when their reactions are being influenced by their own experiences rather than the client's needs. For example, if a therapist has internalized the belief that men should not cry or show weakness, they might unconsciously steer the therapy away from topics that evoke strong emotions, thereby hindering the client's ability to fully process their trauma. By being aware of these internalized beliefs, therapists can better support their clients in challenging societal norms and exploring their full range of emotions.

Furthermore, the relationship between therapist and client is not just a one-way street. It involves a dynamic interplay of "serve and return," where each interaction between therapist and client can bring past distortions and unresolved issues into the therapeutic space. The therapist's responses to the client—whether verbal or non-verbal—can either help the client feel understood and supported, or can reinforce feelings of shame, isolation, and misunderstanding. The therapist's ability to manage countertransference is therefore essential in maintaining a therapeutic environment that is conducive to healing.

Shame and isolation are often central experiences for male survivors of sexual trauma. These emotions can be deeply ingrained, shaped by both the trauma itself and by societal expectations that men should be invulnerable. In therapy, male survivors may struggle to express these feelings, fearing judgment or rejection. Therapists, too, may have their own experiences with shame, which can be triggered by the client's disclosures. If a therapist has not fully addressed their own shame, they may project this onto the client, leading to subtle judgments or discomfort that the client can perceive. This can result in the client feeling even more isolated and misunderstood.

To navigate this complex terrain, therapists must be vigilant in recognizing when countertransference is at play. This requires a deep level of self-awareness and a commitment to ongoing self-reflection. It also involves a willingness to engage in personal therapy or supervision to explore unresolved issues that may be influencing the therapeutic process. By doing so, therapists can better manage their emotional responses and avoid projecting their own issues onto the client.

In addition to self-awareness, understanding the dynamics of safety within the therapeutic relationship is crucial. For male survivors, creating a sense of safety is often a prerequisite for exploring traumatic experiences. This involves not only physical safety but also emotional safety—creating an environment where the client feels comfortable expressing vulnerability without fear of judgment. Therapists must be mindful of how their own unresolved issues, particularly around shame and vulnerability, might affect the client's sense of safety. For instance, if a therapist struggles with vulnerability in their own life, they might unintentionally discourage the client from exploring similar feelings, thereby limiting the depth of the therapeutic work.

The concept of safety is closely tied to the therapist's ability to manage countertransference. When therapists are aware of their own vulnerabilities and biases, they are better equipped to create a therapeutic environment that feels safe and supportive for the client. This might involve actively challenging their own beliefs about masculinity, being open to the full range of the client's emotional experiences, and providing a non-judgmental space where the client can explore their trauma.

The therapeutic relationship, when managed with care and awareness, can become a powerful tool for healing. It provides a space where male survivors can challenge societal norms, explore their vulnerabilities, and work through their trauma in a supportive and understanding environment. However, this process requires the therapist to be constantly attuned to their own internal world, recognizing when countertransference is at play and taking steps to manage it effectively.

In the context of working with male survivors, the therapist's ability to recognize and manage countertransference is particularly important given the societal expectations around masculinity. These expectations can create unique challenges in therapy, both for the client and the therapist. For example, a therapist might unconsciously expect a male client to be less emotional or more self-reliant, which could hinder the client's ability to express their true feelings. Alternatively, a therapist might feel drawn to protect or rescue the client, which could stem from their own unresolved issues around caregiving or vulnerability. In either case, the therapist's countertransference can interfere with the therapeutic process if not properly managed.

To effectively manage countertransference, therapists must be willing to engage in ongoing self-reflection and personal growth. This process involves not only recognizing their own biases and emotional triggers but also actively working to address them. For example, a therapist who has a strong inclination toward maintaining a positive outlook might find themselves struggling with the temptation to avoid or downplay the more painful and negative emotions that arise in therapy. This tendency could lead them to prematurely shift towards meaning-making or resolution, bypassing the crucial integration of intense feelings that is necessary for true healing.

If a therapist recognizes that they have an internal bias toward positivity—perhaps as a coping mechanism in their own life—they may find it challenging to sit with a client's distress or despair. This discomfort might manifest as an urge to redirect the conversation towards more hopeful or solution-focused topics before the client has fully processed their emotions. In such cases, it becomes essential for the therapist to explore these tendencies in their own therapy or through supervision. By doing so, they can gain a deeper understanding of how their need for positivity might be affecting their ability to fully engage with the client's emotional experience.

Through this self-exploration, the therapist can learn to tolerate the discomfort of intense emotions and resist the urge to bypass them. This enables them to remain present with the client during difficult moments, providing the space necessary for the client to fully experience and integrate their feelings before moving towards meaning-making. By confronting and addressing their own biases, therapists can better support their clients in navigating the complex emotional landscapes of trauma and recovery.

In addition to self-reflection, therapists can benefit from creating a supportive professional network that includes supervision, peer consultation, and continuing education. These resources can provide valuable insights and feedback, helping therapists to recognize and manage countertransference more effectively. Supervision, in particular, can offer a space for therapists to explore their countertransference reactions in a supportive and non-judgmental environment, allowing them to gain a deeper understanding of how these reactions are influencing their work.

Ultimately, the goal of managing countertransference is to create a therapeutic environment that is conducive to healing. This involves not only recognizing and addressing the therapist's own emotional responses but also actively working to create a space where the client feels understood, supported, and safe. By doing so, therapists can help male survivors to navigate their trauma, challenge societal norms, and explore their full range of emotions, leading to a more authentic and meaningful healing process.

In conclusion, countertransference is a critical dynamic in the therapeutic process with male survivors of sexual interpersonal trauma. It represents the therapist's emotional and cognitive responses to the client, which can be influenced by the therapist's own experiences, beliefs, and unresolved issues. Understanding and managing countertransference is essential in providing effective and compassionate care, particularly given the societal expectations around masculinity that can complicate the therapeutic process.

By engaging in ongoing self-reflection, seeking supervision, and actively working to address their own biases and emotional triggers, therapists can create a therapeutic environment that supports healing and recovery for male survivors. The shiny object of countertransference, while potentially distracting, can be managed with awareness and intentionality, allowing the therapist to remain focused on the client's needs and the healing journey.

In the therapeutic journey with male survivors of sexual interpersonal trauma, the connection between therapist and survivor is not just important—it is the very foundation upon which healing occurs. As therapists, we must acknowledge our humanity and recognize that we do not always show up perfectly for our clients. This recognition is vital, as it opens the door to self-awareness and growth, allowing us to better support the survivors in their journey toward recovery. Healing, after all, always happens within the context of a relationship; it cannot be accomplished in isolation.

To navigate the complexities of this therapeutic relationship, I have identified fifteen key characteristics that serve as guardrails, guiding therapists in how they show up to provide the most effective healing mechanisms for survivors. These characteristics are not only practical tools but also embody the concept of being a "fair witness"—a stable and trustworthy presence that survivors can rely on, especially when a leap of faith is required to confront vulnerability and trauma.

Among these fifteen attributes, authenticity stands out as the thread that weaves through the entire therapeutic process. Authenticity is critical because it is the very element that offenders manipulate to exploit their victims. Offenders often create a facade of trustworthiness and sincerity, using it to gain control over their victims. This manipulation of authenticity creates deep wounds and makes it incredibly difficult for survivors to trust again.

However, in the therapeutic environment, authenticity serves the opposite purpose. It becomes the foundation upon which trust is rebuilt, allowing survivors to take the leap of faith necessary to engage fully in the healing process. Authenticity in therapy helps survivors unravel the manipulation they have experienced, disentangling self-blame, shame, fear, and conflicted loyalties, and fostering genuine connections with others.

The following chapters will delve into each of these fifteen attributes in detail, exploring how they can be utilized in the therapeutic environment to create a safe and supportive space for healing. These attributes include:

- **Authenticity**: Helping survivors differentiate between manipulation and genuine relationships, and supporting them in rebuilding trust.
- **Ability to Contain the Story**: Providing a safe space where survivors feel heard and held without judgment.
- **Confidentiality**: Ensuring that the therapeutic space remains secure and private, allowing survivors to share openly.
- **Maintaining Effective Boundaries**: Establishing clear emotional, physical, and mental boundaries that protect both therapist and client.
- **Use of Self-Disclosure**: Sharing personal experiences appropriately to create relatability and deepen the therapeutic connection.
- **Curiosity and Non-Judgmental Attitude**: Approaching the survivor's behavior with curiosity, recognizing biases, and avoiding judgment.

- **Recognizing the Shiny Object**: Identifying and managing distractions or emotional triggers that might detract from the therapeutic focus.
- **Humility**: Acknowledging the therapist's limitations and being open to learning and growth.
- **Ability to Challenge Belief with Compassion**: Gently challenging distorted beliefs held by the survivor, encouraging them to explore new perspectives while honoring their emotional experiences.
- **Recognizing Countertransference**: Being aware of the therapist's emotional reactions and ensuring they do not interfere with the client's healing.
- **Formulating Hypotheses**: Developing thoughtful hypotheses to connect the dots between the survivor's experiences and behaviors.
- **Ability to Repair Ruptures**: Addressing and repairing any disruptions or misunderstandings in the therapeutic relationship.
- **Reliability and Predictability**: Being a consistent and dependable presence for the survivor.
- **Ability to Be Present**: Offering full presence and attunement, mirroring the survivor's experiences and validating their reality.
- **Ability to Be Optimistic**: Maintaining hope for the survivor's potential for healing, fostering resilience, and encouraging the belief that positive change is possible.

These characteristics are crucial not only for guiding the therapeutic relationship but also for differentiating it from the harmful dynamics that survivors experienced with their offenders.

For male survivors, the mere act of engaging in a vulnerable relationship can be triggering, which is why authenticity is emphasized throughout the narrative. It is the element that, when used with integrity, allows survivors to rediscover their ability to trust and to heal within the context of a safe, supportive relationship.

As we explore these attributes in the coming chapters, we will also examine the similarities between the therapeutic relationship and the dynamics with the offender, while highlighting how the therapeutic relationship differs fundamentally in its intention and impact. By understanding and implementing these fifteen characteristics, therapists can create an environment where male survivors feel empowered to confront their trauma, rebuild their sense of self, and take the necessary steps toward healing.

Chapter 11

AUTHENTICITY-THE CORNERSTONE OF THE THERAPEUTIC RELATIONSHIP

In the sacred space of the therapy room, where unspoken words are laden with vulnerability, and untold stories wait to be shared, authenticity takes on profound significance. It is here, amidst the delicate dance between therapist and client, that authenticity reveals its transformative power. As therapists, our commitment to authenticity is not just about being genuine with our clients—it is the very foundation upon which the therapeutic relationship is built, allowing healing to take place within the context of trust, safety, and mutual respect.

Authenticity in therapy is not merely a professional obligation; it is an essential element of the recovery process for survivors of interpersonal sexual trauma. How we present ourselves as therapists—whether we are genuine, transparent, and fully present—can have a significant impact on our clients' ability to heal. Authenticity involves showing up in the therapy room without pretense, without a script, and without the need to hide behind a professional facade. It means being true to who we are, acknowledging our own vulnerabilities, and modeling healthy relational behaviors for our clients.

For survivors of sexual trauma, especially men, authenticity is crucial. Many male survivors struggle with forming and maintaining authentic relationships due to unresolved interpersonal trauma.

They may have learned to protect themselves by masking their true selves, avoiding vulnerability, and adhering to societal expectations of stoicism and emotional restraint. In therapy, they may initially approach the therapeutic relationship with skepticism, unsure if they can trust the therapist enough to reveal their deepest wounds. This is where the therapist's authenticity becomes a beacon of hope, signaling that it is safe to be vulnerable, to be seen, and to be heard.

In today's society, men face unique challenges in cultivating authenticity. They are often socialized to believe that showing emotion is a sign of weakness, and they may fear that revealing their true selves will lead to rejection or ridicule. These fears are compounded for those who have experienced trauma, where the very essence of trust and authenticity was exploited by their abuser. The goal of therapy, therefore, is to help these men reconnect with their authentic selves, to understand that their experiences are valid, and to learn that they can form healthy, fulfilling connections once again.

The intersection of authenticity and judgment is a delicate balance in the therapeutic process. Authenticity requires a deep level of self-awareness, where the therapist must be fully present and genuine, offering an unfiltered version of themselves to the client. However, judgment, often rooted in personal biases and cultural conditioning, can create a barrier to this authenticity. When we judge, we impose a set of expectations or standards that can inhibit our ability to truly connect with our clients. Judgment fosters a facade, both for the therapist and the client, where the true self is masked, and the therapeutic relationship becomes a space of conformity rather than genuine interaction.

It is crucial for therapists to acknowledge that their biases and judgments do not exist in a vacuum—they are shaped by their experiences within the broader culture and their personal histories. Whether it is societal norms, cultural expectations, or past personal experiences, these influences can unconsciously seep into the therapeutic space, distorting the therapist's ability to remain authentic. Recognizing and confronting these biases is essential for maintaining authenticity. By admitting our judgments and the origins of our biases, we can dismantle the facades they create and move toward a more genuine, open, and healing relationship with our clients. This process not only deepens the therapeutic connection but also models for clients how to confront and overcome their judgments, leading to more authentic relationships in their own lives.

As therapists, we must recognize that authenticity is not a static trait; it is a dynamic process that requires ongoing self-reflection and personal growth. This journey begins with acknowledging our own humanity, our biases, and our emotional triggers. It is crucial to understand that we, too, are susceptible to countertransference—our emotional reactions to the client that may stem from our unresolved issues or personal experiences. If we cannot be fully present for our clients in the way that we know we should, this needs to be explored. Countertransference, when left unchecked, can undermine the therapeutic process and erode the trust that is so vital to healing.

For some therapists, there is a temptation to rely on a script—a predetermined way of interacting with clients that feels safe and controlled. While structure and consistency are important in therapy, they should not come at the expense of authenticity. When we operate from a script, we risk becoming disconnected from the present moment, missing the nuances of the client's experience, and failing to respond in a way that is attuned to their needs. Authenticity, on the other hand, requires us to be fully engaged, to respond to the client from a place of genuine care and understanding, and to allow the therapeutic process to unfold organically.

In "Stranger in a Strange Land" by Robert Heinlein, the concept of the fair witness is introduced as a figure who embodies profound commitment to authenticity and vulnerability. The fair witness, by definition, is someone who observes and reports with complete accuracy and without interpretation, remaining neutral and impartial. This concept offers valuable insights into the therapeutic process. Like the fair witness, the therapist must strive to observe and validate the client's experiences without imposing their interpretations or biases. This stance of neutrality is essential for creating an environment where the client feels seen, heard, and understood without reservation.

The character of Valentine Michael Smith, the protagonist in Heinlein's novel, embodies the essence of authenticity. Raised by Martians, Mike approaches every interaction with a childlike curiosity and a willingness to embrace his truth without reservation. In a pivotal scene, Mike is brought to a court trial where his nature as a fair witness is tested. He is asked to testify about his experiences on Mars, particularly his understanding of love and intimacy. Rather than conforming to the rigid expectations of the court, Mike responds with honesty and vulnerability, sharing his Martian perspective on these deeply human concepts.

Mike's testimony, particularly his discussion of "grokking," which involves a deep understanding and empathy for the inter-connectedness of all things, challenges the court to reconsider their beliefs about love and intimacy. His authenticity and vulnerability serve as a catalyst for transformation, inspiring those around him to question their assumptions and embrace a more compassionate understanding of the human experience.

In the context of therapy, Mike's example is a powerful reminder of the importance of authenticity. When therapists embrace authenticity, they create a safe and supportive environment where clients feel empowered to explore their deepest thoughts and emotions. This process is not about imposing shame or making clients feel judged; rather, it is about holding space for them to confront their truths with courage and openness.

In the therapy room, authenticity is the cornerstone of the therapeutic relationship. It is the unwavering commitment to showing up fully present, genuine, and transparent in every interaction. When a therapist embodies authenticity, they create a safe container where trust can flourish, allowing the client to peel back the layers of their soul and reveal the raw truths that lie beneath. In this sacred space, devoid of judgment or expectation, the therapist assumes the role of the fair witness, seeking to observe and validate the client's experiences without imposing their interpretations or biases.

The journey of authenticity begins with the therapist's willingness to embrace their humanity. This requires a deep commitment to self-awareness and introspection, as the therapist navigates their own biases, insecurities, and vulnerabilities. By acknowledging their imperfections and limitations, the therapist models vulnerability, inviting the client to do the same.

In adopting the role of a fair witness, therapists prepare clients to engage with challenging beliefs from a stance of nonjudgmental support and objective understanding. The fair witness approach ensures that any statements or insights presented to the client are derived strictly from the data they have provided, rather than being influenced by the therapist's own cultural or personal experiences. This method reassures clients that their narratives are being received and evaluated based on their unique context and experiences, fostering a safe space where they can explore and reassess their beliefs without fear of judgment or bias. By clearly communicating that feedback and challenges come solely from the client's own story, therapists help clients feel validated and understood, encouraging them to confront and reframe limiting beliefs with confidence. This objective, data-driven interaction not only strengthens the therapeutic alliance but also empowers clients to trust in the process of their own healing and growth, knowing that their therapist is dedicated to supporting their journey with integrity and authenticity.

As therapists, we must be vigilant in recognizing when our need to maintain a positive outlook or to avoid discomfort leads us to bypass the intense emotions that arise in therapy. Authenticity means being willing to sit with those difficult feelings, both in ourselves and in our clients, and to allow them to be fully expressed and integrated before moving toward meaning-making or resolution. This is where countertransference becomes a critical issue—if we find ourselves unable to be fully present with our clients because we are uncomfortable with the intensity of their emotions, we must explore these reactions in our own therapy or supervision.

When a therapist surrenders to the vulnerability of authenticity, they create a space where the client can explore their truth without fear of judgment or rejection. This space becomes a sanctuary for healing, where the client can shed the masks that they wear to navigate the outside world and reveal their authentic selves in all their complexity. In the absence of expectations, the therapist relinquishes the need to guide or control the client's journey. Instead, they adopt an attitude of curiosity and openness, allowing the client's narrative to unfold organically. This approach honors the client's autonomy, empowering them to take ownership of their healing process and make decisions that align with their values and goals.

The therapist's role as the fair witness is to bear witness to the client's truth with humility and reverence. They resist the urge to intervene or offer unsolicited advice, trusting in the client's inherent wisdom to guide them on their journey. Through active listening and empathic attunement, the therapist validates the client's experiences, affirming their worthiness and dignity as human beings. However, when distortions in the client's narrative interfere with their growth and curiosity, the therapist must gently intervene, offering guidance without imposing their agenda.

In the sacred dance of authenticity and the fair witness, the therapist and client co-create a narrative of healing and transformation. Together, they traverse the landscape of the soul, navigating the rocky terrain of trauma and the fertile soil of resilience. With each step, they move closer to wholeness, embracing the full spectrum of human experience with courage and grace.

As the therapy journey unfolds, the therapist remains anchored in the principles of authenticity and the fair witness, guiding the client with empathy and compassion. They recognize that healing is not a linear process but a messy, beautiful journey of self-discovery and self-acceptance. In the end, the therapist emerges not as a savior or a fixer, but as a fellow traveler on the path to healing.

In the tapestry of therapy, authenticity and the fair witness are threads that weave together to create a masterpiece of human connection and transformation. In the sacred space of the therapy room, where vulnerability reigns supreme, they become guiding stars, illuminating the path to healing and wholeness. And in the quiet moments between words, they whisper a truth as old as time—that in the presence of authenticity, anything is possible.

This chapter, and the subsequent exploration of the fifteen characteristics that serve as guardrails in the therapeutic relationship, underscores the centrality of authenticity in the healing process. As we delve deeper into each attribute, we will explore how they can be utilized to create a therapeutic environment that not only supports the survivor's recovery but also fosters the growth of genuine, authentic relationships. The therapist's role is to provide the safe, authentic space where survivors can reclaim their voices, rebuild their trust, and take the necessary steps toward a life of connection, fulfillment, and healing.

HOLDING SPACE WITH AUTHENTICITY: THE THERAPIST'S IMPACT ON JOHN'S HEALING PROCESS

John had always been a man of dual lives. By day, he was a successful businessman, the kind of person others admired for his sharp mind and unwavering control. He had built a thriving company from the ground up, earning respect and recognition in his industry. But beneath this polished exterior, John harbored a secret life, one that he kept meticulously hidden from the world. His success in business was matched by his ability to compartmentalize his personal life, particularly his use of sex workers as a way to act out and exert control over his sexual desires.

This secret life was something John never allowed to intersect with his public persona. The shame he felt about these actions was immense, but rather than confront it, he buried it deep within himself. He maintained a strict separation between his professional success and his personal indulgences, convincing himself that these two worlds could never collide. This closed-minded approach kept him safe—or so he thought—from the vulnerability of letting anyone truly see the full picture of who he was.

John's need for control extended to every aspect of his life, including his emotions. He had long used shame as a tool to keep his behaviors in check, believing that if he could just judge himself harshly enough, he could prevent these behaviors from spiraling out of control. But this strategy had a dark side. The more John relied on shame to suppress his actions, the more disconnected he became from understanding the deeper reasons behind them. Rather than exploring the roots of his behavior from a place of curiosity and self-compassion, he doubled down on his efforts to keep his two worlds separate, further entrenching his closed-minded thinking.

As John began therapy, he brought with him this rigid mindset, along with the belief that his therapist would never truly understand him if she knew the full extent of his actions. He had spent years perfecting the art of secrecy, and the thought of exposing his vulnerabilities—even in a therapeutic setting—was terrifying.

But as his therapist, I knew that to help John, I had to meet him where he was, and that required a level of authenticity and vulnerability that I, too, had struggled with. I had always prided myself on maintaining a positive outlook, often using this positivity as a shield to avoid sitting in the discomfort of difficult emotions. This tendency, which I had come to recognize as toxic positivity, sometimes led me to rush through the more painful aspects of therapy, pushing for solutions and silver linings before my clients were ready to move on.

In one session, after sensing John's hesitation to delve into the darker parts of his life, I decided to take a risk and share a bit of my own struggle. I told John about my tendency to avoid discomfort by leaning into positivity too quickly, and how I had come to realize that this approach, while well-intentioned, could sometimes undermine the therapeutic process. I admitted that I had to consciously work on staying present with my clients in their most painful moments, resisting the urge to fix or reframe their experiences too soon.

John listened intently, and I could see the wheels turning in his mind. My disclosure seemed to strike a chord with him, and for the first time, I saw a crack in the armor he had so carefully constructed. Knowing that even I, his therapist, struggled with staying in difficult emotional spaces helped him feel less alone in his journey. It also gave him permission to start exploring his own emotions without immediately retreating into shame or judgment.

Over time, John began to open up about his secret life, revealing the extent of his use of sex workers and the shame that came with it. He confessed that he had always seen this part of his life as something separate from who he truly was—as if these actions were just a dark shadow he could keep hidden, rather than an integral part of his experience that needed to be understood.

As we worked together, John started to see that his behavior was not simply something to be judged and suppressed, but a manifestation of deeper, unresolved trauma. He began to explore the reasons why he sought control in these ways, recognizing how his need for secrecy and compartmentalization stemmed from a fear of vulnerability and a profound mistrust in the world around him. By bringing these hidden parts of himself into the light, John was able to start the process of integrating his experiences, rather than keeping them locked away in separate compartments of his mind.

The shift was slow, but it was real. John's rigid, closed-minded thinking began to soften as he learned to approach his behaviors with curiosity rather than condemnation. He started to understand that his use of shame as a tool for control was not only ineffective but harmful, preventing him from accessing the deeper emotions that needed to be addressed for true healing to occur.

Throughout this process, I also found myself changing. By holding space for John's difficult emotions without rushing to find a positive spin, I discovered a new depth in my own capacity as a therapist. My commitment to authenticity—both in acknowledging my own struggles and in creating a space where John could be fully himself—allowed us both to grow in unexpected ways.

John's journey was far from easy, and the road to healing required him to confront parts of himself that he had long tried to ignore. But by embracing authenticity and vulnerability, both in himself and in our therapeutic relationship, he was able to break free from the cycle of shame and secrecy that had kept him trapped for so long. As he began to integrate the different aspects of his life, John found a new sense of freedom—a freedom to be fully himself, without the need for masks or compartments. And in doing so, he started to build a life that was not only successful but also authentic, honest, and whole.

Chapter 12

BEYOND LISTENING: THE ART OF CONTAINING THE STORY IN THE THERAPEUTIC RELATIONSHIP

Trauma survivors often carry a profound fear that others will not be able to handle the weight of their stories. This fear is rooted in the belief that sharing their experiences will lead to judgment, shame, or rejection. For many, the very thought of revealing the depths of their trauma is paralyzing, as they worry that others, including therapists, may be overwhelmed by the intensity of their narratives. The essence of the therapeutic process, particularly in trauma work, lies in the therapist's ability to effectively contain these stories, providing a safe space where survivors can gradually reveal their experiences, layer by layer.

The process of sharing a trauma narrative in therapy often begins with tentative steps. Survivors may start by disclosing small fragments of their story, carefully observing the therapist's response to gauge whether it is safe to proceed. These initial disclosures serve as tests, allowing the survivor to assess whether the therapist can emotionally hold and tolerate their story. It is only when they feel assured that the therapist can handle the weight of their experiences that they begin to share more deeply. This gradual revelation is crucial, as it helps survivors build trust and confidence in the therapeutic relationship, knowing that they can be co-regulated as they share the most painful parts of their past.

One of the fifteen characteristics essential to the therapeutic process is the therapist's ability to contain the story. This skill involves more than just listening; it requires the therapist to hold the survivor's narrative with empathy, without being overwhelmed or passing judgment. The ability to contain the story effectively is critical because many trauma survivors struggle with the belief that others—particularly those in positions of trust, like therapists—are incapable of emotionally handling their narratives. This fear is deeply rooted in their past experiences, where vulnerability may have been met with betrayal, invalidation, or outright harm.

As survivors tentatively disclose their trauma, they often fear that revealing too much too soon will lead to rejection or that the listener will be emotionally damaged by what they hear. This fear can prevent them from fully engaging in the therapeutic process, keeping them trapped in a cycle of silence and self-blame. The therapist's role is to create a space where the survivor feels safe enough to share their story at their own pace, knowing that they will not be judged or rejected. This involves not only providing reassurance but also demonstrating, through consistent and compassionate presence, that the therapist can indeed handle whatever is shared.

The ability to contain a client's story is a crucial function in the therapeutic process, especially when working with trauma survivors. When clients begin to share their trauma, it's not just about recounting events—it's also about processing the deeply embedded emotions and beliefs tied to those experiences. Many survivors, particularly those who have endured relational trauma, carry intense feelings of shame and fear. They may have internalized the belief that their trauma makes them defective or unworthy of love and support. This belief can be so powerful that it leads them to project their fears onto the therapist, worrying that their story will be too overwhelming, even for a professional.

In this context, the therapist's role in containing the story becomes paramount. Clients need to trust that their narrative can be held without judgment or rejection. This trust is often challenged by the protective mechanisms of PTSD, where avoidance serves as a way to keep overwhelming emotions at bay. Clients might avoid delving into their trauma because they fear that once they start feeling those buried emotions, they won't be able to stop or contain them. This avoidance often manifests as a projection, where clients doubt the therapist's ability to handle their story, when in reality, it's their own fear of losing control that underlies this belief.

As therapists, we must engage in a delicate balance—gently encouraging clients to share their experiences while ensuring they feel safe and contained. The act of containing the story means providing a space where clients can gradually explore their emotions, knowing they won't be judged or abandoned. It's about helping them understand that feeling deeply doesn't equate to losing control, but rather, it's a step toward healing. By consistently holding and containing their stories, we can help clients slowly dismantle their avoidance patterns, empowering them to confront their trauma at a pace that feels manageable and secure. Through this process, we challenge the deeply rooted beliefs of defectiveness and unworthiness, allowing clients to see that their story is not too much to bear and that they are deserving of support and compassion.

Many therapists may idealize the notion that allowing the client to dictate the pace of exploring their trauma narrative is necessary to keep the situation under control. However, as therapists, we must recognize the primary function of PTSD, particularly the role of avoidance, and ensure that we do not become complicit in this avoidance dance with the client. Avoidance is a natural protective mechanism in PTSD, but if left unaddressed, it can hinder the therapeutic process and prevent meaningful progress.

I often hear therapists in supervision express concerns that their clients are telling them they are not ready to explore the trauma narrative. This raises an important question: How do we distinguish between being complicit in the client's avoidance and respecting their need to pace the therapy? The answer lies in our ability to contain the story effectively. Containing the story involves more than just passively waiting for the client to be ready; it requires us to actively engage with the trauma narrative in a way that gently challenges avoidance without overwhelming the client.

Identifying the "port of entry" into the trauma narrative becomes imperative in this context. The port of entry is the point at which the trauma narrative begins to emerge, often in subtle or indirect ways. By recognizing these moments and using them to lean into the story, we can guide the client away from avoidance and toward a deeper exploration of their experiences. This approach helps the client understand that the therapist is not afraid of the trauma narrative and can handle its full weight. It also demonstrates that the therapist can see how the trauma leaks out into the client's current life and across their life span.

By carefully containing the story and strategically identifying the port of entry, we create a therapeutic environment where the client feels supported in confronting their trauma. This approach ensures that we are not merely colluding with avoidance but are instead fostering a space where the client can safely and gradually explore their trauma at a pace that balances both their readiness and the need to move beyond avoidance. This nuanced dance between pacing and confronting the trauma narrative is critical in helping the client reclaim their story and integrate their experiences in a meaningful way.

However, the process of externalizing and sharing their experiences can be profoundly healing. When survivors begin to see that their therapist can hold and tolerate their trauma narrative, they start to challenge the belief that their story is too overwhelming. This validation helps to dismantle the narrative of defectiveness and allows survivors to engage more deeply in the therapeutic process.

One of the core elements of containing the story is the understanding that it will be revealed in layers. Survivors need to know that they can trust the therapist to remain steady and supportive as they peel back the layers of their experiences. This process requires the therapist to be fully present, attuned, and responsive, providing the necessary co-regulation that helps the survivor navigate the intense emotions that surface as they delve deeper into their story.

As survivors move from the cognitive retelling of their trauma to the affective processing of their emotions, the therapeutic space becomes a crucible for transformation. This transition is pivotal in the healing journey, as it allows survivors to confront and process the emotional pain, fear, and shame that have long been buried beneath the surface. However, this process is often hindered by the survivor's own avoidance strategies—patterns of behavior that have developed as coping mechanisms in response to trauma.

Avoidance is a common symptom of trauma, serving as a way to protect oneself from the overwhelming emotions associated with traumatic memories. Survivors may avoid certain thoughts, feelings, or situations that trigger reminders of their trauma. In therapy, this avoidance can manifest as reluctance to fully engage with the therapeutic process, using the excuse that others cannot handle their story as a convenient justification for staying silent. This avoidance not only perpetuates the narrative of defectiveness but also reinforces the belief that recovery is unattainable because they are irreparably broken.

The role of the therapist in this context is to gently challenge these avoidance behaviors while respecting the survivor's pace. By providing a safe and nonjudgmental space, the therapist can help the survivor explore the underlying reasons for their avoidance and begin to confront the emotions they have been avoiding. This process requires the therapist to be patient and compassionate, offering consistent support and validation as the survivor begins to open up.

Another critical aspect of this process is the therapist's ability to manage their own countertransference. Countertransference refers to the therapist's emotional reactions to the client, which are often shaped by the therapist's own experiences and beliefs. If a therapist has unresolved issues related to trauma or if they hold unconscious biases about trauma survivors, these can significantly impact their ability to contain the client's story effectively. For example, a therapist who struggles with their own fear of vulnerability may unconsciously project this fear onto the client, leading to a reluctance to fully engage with the survivor's narrative.

Managing countertransference requires ongoing self-reflection and a commitment to personal growth. Therapists must be aware of their own emotional responses and how these may influence their interactions with clients. This awareness allows the therapist to remain present and attuned, providing the necessary containment for the survivor's story without letting their own issues interfere with the therapeutic process.

The concept of containment is closely linked to the idea of co-regulation—the process by which one person's emotional state influences and is influenced by another's. In the therapeutic context, co-regulation occurs when the therapist's calm, grounded presence helps the survivor manage their emotional responses. This is particularly important when working with trauma survivors, who may struggle to regulate their emotions due to the impact of trauma on their nervous system. By maintaining a steady, compassionate presence, the therapist can help the survivor feel safe enough to explore their emotions without becoming overwhelmed.

However, creating this environment of safety and containment also requires the therapist to confront their own vulnerabilities. In my work with trauma survivors, I have found that one of my own challenges has been a tendency toward toxic positivity—an inclination to focus on the positive aspects of a situation while minimizing or avoiding the more difficult emotions. This tendency, while well-intentioned, can create a barrier to authentic connection and hinder the therapeutic process. Survivors need to feel that their pain is recognized and validated, not glossed over in an effort to move toward resolution too quickly.

The ability to contain the story effectively is not just about listening; it is about being fully present and attuned to the survivor's needs. It is about creating a space where the survivor feels safe enough to share their story, knowing that it will be held with care and compassion. This process is essential for helping survivors move beyond the cognitive aspects of their trauma and into the deeper, emotional layers that must be processed for healing to occur.

When working with clients who have experienced interpersonal abuse, particularly those who attempted to tell their story as children but were not believed, an additional layer of complexity arises in the therapeutic process. The experience of not being believed—whether by those around them or even by their own internal belief system—can profoundly shape how they navigate their narrative as adults. This history of disbelief often contributes to the layering of disclosures in therapy, where clients may reveal their story gradually, testing the waters to see if they will finally be heard and validated.

As therapists, it is crucial to consider this element of disbelief as we help clients contain and process their stories. The disbelief they encountered as children can lead to deep-seated doubts about the validity of their own experiences, making it difficult for them to fully embrace and articulate their truth. Part of our role is to help clients differentiate between what can be externally validated as fact and what is true to them based on their lived experience. Both forms of truth are valid and essential in the healing process, even if they cannot be corroborated by others.

In my experience as a therapist, I have often encountered clients who feel compelled to convince me that their story is true. They may repeat a portion of the story emphatically, almost as if they are trying to make me understand or believe it. This compulsion often stems from the deep wound of having been dismissed or disbelieved in the past. It is a way of seeking the validation they were denied as children. In these moments, it is crucial for the therapist to affirm that they believe the client. This affirmation is not just a therapeutic tool but a fundamental part of the containment of the story. It reassures the client that their narrative is safe within the therapeutic space, and that their experiences are valid and worthy of acknowledgment.

Helping clients understand the function of their story becomes key to their healing journey. Telling their story is not just an act of sharing; it is a therapeutic process that can help regulate the nervous system and reduce the anxiety that often accompanies trauma. By gradually leaning into their story and exploring the reactions it evokes, clients can begin to dismantle the compulsive repetition of trauma-related behaviors and thoughts. This process of telling and retelling the story, in layers and at their own pace, allows clients to re-examine their experiences, validate their emotions, and ultimately dissipate the power that these unresolved narratives hold over their lives.

Therapists must also be attuned to the significance of this process for the client's sense of self. For many survivors, particularly those who were dismissed or disbelieved as children, being able to tell their story and have it contained with respect and belief is profoundly healing. It validates their experiences and helps to rebuild the trust that was shattered in their formative years. By providing a safe space for these layered disclosures and affirming the client's truth, therapists can support clients in reclaiming their narrative, fostering a sense of empowerment, and facilitating the healing of deep emotional wounds.

Ultimately, the therapist's ability to contain the story is a crucial component of the therapeutic process, especially when working with trauma survivors. This skill involves managing countertransference, providing co-regulation, and maintaining a steady, compassionate presence that allows the survivor to gradually reveal their experiences. A key aspect of this process is identifying the "port of entry" into the trauma narrative—those moments when the story begins to surface, often in subtle or indirect ways. By recognizing and leaning into these points of entry, therapists can gently guide clients away from avoidance and deeper into their narrative. Creating a safe, nonjudgmental space where the therapist is authentically present and vulnerable allows the client to feel secure enough to confront their fears. This approach not only helps clients challenge avoidance behaviors but also empowers them to reclaim their stories and lives. Through a commitment to self-awareness, therapists can support their clients in this delicate dance, fostering a path toward healing and integration.

FROM DISTRACTION TO DISCOVERY: USING THE SHINY OBJECT TO CONTAIN AND EXPLORE JOHN'S HIDDEN NARRATIVE

John had always prided himself on his work ethic, a trait he had learned early on from his stepfather. This drive to succeed and the relentless pursuit of perfection had served him well in his career, helping him build a successful business from the ground up. However, beneath this veneer of success lay a complex web of unresolved trauma, secrecy, and a deep-seated need for control—elements that were beginning to unravel his personal life, particularly his relationship with his wife.

John's stepfather had been a significant influence in his life, teaching him the value of hard work and discipline. On the surface, these lessons seemed positive, shaping John into the driven and accomplished man he had become. But these same lessons were intertwined with a darker reality: his stepfather's abuse and the secrecy that surrounded it. The positive trait of work ethic was inextricably linked to the abusive environment in which John grew up. This connection between work and worthiness became a crucial "port of entry" in therapy, a way to explore how John's current behaviors were rooted in his past experiences.

As we delved into this port of entry, John began to confront the painful memories of his childhood. He had long suspected that his mother was aware of the abuse but chose to do nothing about it, a realization that had left him with a deep sense of betrayal and abandonment. This belief—that the person who should have protected him had turned a blind eye—shaped his future relationships. It was no coincidence that John had married a woman who was incredibly attuned to the needs of their children, and to John himself. Her attunement, while comforting on one level, often felt suffocating to John, triggering memories of the control and powerlessness he felt as a child.

In therapy, we explored how this dynamic with his wife was another port of entry into his trauma narrative. The same attunement that drew him to his wife now felt like control, a reminder of his childhood experiences where his autonomy was stripped away. This insight helped John see how his need for control, which served him so well in business, was actually a defense mechanism developed in response to his early trauma. His relentless pursuit of success and his hyperfixation on work were not just about ambition—they were about proving his worth, about believing that if he worked hard enough, his stepfather would finally see value in him beyond the abuse.

But this need to perform and be seen was not just about earning approval; it was also about distraction. By immersing himself in work, John could avoid confronting the painful memories of his past. This avoidance played out in other areas of his life as well, particularly in his use of sex workers. Amidst all of John's struggles, there was one glaring issue that finally drove him into therapy: his compulsive use of sex workers. On the surface, it seemed like the betrayal of his marriage was the primary problem, the catalyst that threatened to unravel everything he had worked so hard to build—his life, his relationship, his work, his family. But as we peeled back the layers, it became clear that the sex addiction was a "shiny object," a distraction from the deeper issues at play. It wasn't just about the act of betrayal; it was about the underlying fear of vulnerability and the avoidance of pain that had plagued him for years. The addiction provided a temporary escape, a way to exert control over one part of his life when other areas felt too overwhelming. Yet, this same escape was leading him down a path of destruction, jeopardizing everything he held dear.

As we continued to explore these ports of entry, it became clear that John's hyperfixation on control, which had paid off so well in his business, was interfering with his ability to be vulnerable and authentic in his marriage. His fear of vulnerability was deeply tied to his childhood experiences—the secrecy, the abuse, and the belief that his worth was contingent on his performance. This fear led him to seek out relationships where he could maintain control, even if it meant distancing himself from genuine intimacy. The transactional nature of these encounters allowed him to maintain control while avoiding the vulnerability required in his relationship with his wife. It was a way to keep his two worlds separate, to compartmentalize his life so that the shame and pain of his past would not interfere with the image of success he had built.

In therapy, my role was to contain John's story, to provide a space where these complex and painful connections could be explored without judgment or rejection. I had to demonstrate to John that his story could be held, no matter how dark or complicated, and that he would not be abandoned for revealing it. By identifying and leaning into these ports of entry, we were able to move past the surface-level symptoms of his behavior and address the underlying trauma that drove them. I also needed to ensure that as these feelings surfaced, John felt co-regulated, supported, and understood—disrupting his long-held perception that revealing his imperfections would lead to rejection or loss of control.

As John started to confront these difficult truths, he began to realize that the same qualities that made him successful in business were preventing him from experiencing true intimacy in his personal life. The work ethic he had inherited from his stepfather, while valuable, was also a constant reminder of the conditions under which it was learned. His drive to succeed, his need for control, and his avoidance of vulnerability were all rooted in a desire to be valued in ways that his stepfather never did.

Through our work together, John began to see that his story could be told, that it could be contained, and that it did not need to define him. By exploring these ports of entry, we were able to connect the dots between his past and his present, allowing him to begin the process of healing. He started to understand that his worth was not tied to his performance, that he could be vulnerable without losing control, and that his relationships could be based on authenticity rather than avoidance.

John's journey in therapy was not an easy one, but it was transformative. By acknowledging the intersections of his work ethic, his trauma, and his need for control, he began to reclaim his story. He learned that the qualities that had once protected him could also be transformed into strengths that supported his healing. And in doing so, John moved closer to the life he truly wanted— one where he could be successful, loved, and, most importantly, authentically himself.

Chapter 13

CREATING A SAFE SPACE: THE ROLE OF CONFIDENTIALITY IN TRAUMA RECOVERY

Confidentiality is one of the bedrocks of the therapeutic process, particularly when working with clients who have experienced trauma. It forms the foundation of trust, providing clients with the assurance that their most vulnerable and painful experiences will be held securely, without fear of judgment or exposure. However, when working with collateral partners such as spouses, family members, employers, or other support systems, the concept of confidentiality becomes even more complex. Balancing the need for confidentiality with the demands of these external relationships requires careful navigation to ensure the client's safety and the integrity of the therapeutic process.

In therapy, the client's sense of safety is paramount. Without a firm foundation of trust, clients are unlikely to fully engage in the therapeutic process, especially when it involves delving into painful or traumatic experiences. Confidentiality is what allows clients to feel safe enough to open up, knowing that what they share in the therapy room will not be disclosed to others without their explicit consent. This confidentiality is not just a matter of ethics; it is a crucial element that fosters a sense of control and empowerment for the client.

When collateral partners are involved, maintaining this confidentiality can become a delicate balancing act. Clients often come to therapy at the urging or in the context of their relationships with spouses, family members, or even employers. These relationships can play a significant role in the client's life, and in some cases, their involvement can be beneficial to the therapeutic process. But the involvement of these external parties also brings up significant challenges, particularly when it comes to maintaining the client's confidentiality and ensuring their safety.

For clients who have experienced relational trauma, confidentiality takes on even greater significance. Trust has often been shattered in these relationships, leaving clients wary of sharing their stories with anyone, including their therapist. In such cases, the assurance of confidentiality is not just a professional obligation; it is a lifeline that helps rebuild the client's capacity to trust. But when collateral partners are involved, the boundaries of confidentiality can become blurred, raising complex ethical and therapeutic questions.

One of the most challenging aspects of working with collateral partners is navigating the expectations and pressures that these individuals may bring into the therapeutic space. Spouses, family members, or employers may have their own agendas, concerns, or desires for the therapy's outcome, which may not always align with the client's needs or best interests. As a therapist, it is essential to remain attuned to these dynamics and to prioritize the client's confidentiality and safety above all else.

When a client is referred to therapy by a collateral partner, particularly an employer or a spouse, there may be an implicit or explicit expectation that the therapist will share information about the client's progress or disclosures. However, therapists must be vigilant in upholding the boundaries of confidentiality. Even when there is pressure from collateral partners to disclose information, the therapist's primary responsibility is to the client and to maintaining the integrity of the therapeutic process.

In therapy, it is crucial to distinguish between collateral therapy and couples therapy, as they serve different purposes. In collateral therapy, other individuals, such as family members or friends, may be involved to enhance the therapeutic relationship and provide additional context or support for the primary client. The focus remains on the individual's healing, and the involvement of others is secondary to the main therapeutic goals. Confidentiality in collateral therapy is carefully managed to maintain the trust between the therapist and the client, with clear boundaries about what information can be shared.

In couples therapy, however, both partners are directly involved, and the focus shifts to the relationship itself. Here, the therapeutic goal is to address issues that affect the couple as a unit. Navigating confidentiality in couples therapy requires even greater intentionality, particularly when sharing sensitive information with the survivor's partner. The therapist must balance transparency with the need to protect the relationship. If certain disclosures risk creating disconnection between partners, the therapist must carefully consider how to handle that information while maintaining the overall goal of fostering connection and healing within the relationship.

When working with collateral partners, such as spouses, family members, or close friends, the concepts of secrecy and privacy take on critical importance. Clients who have experienced relational trauma often grapple with deep-seated shame, which can keep their true stories hidden under layers of secrecy. However, as they progress in therapy and begin to move out of the shame that once bound them, they may feel a growing desire to share their narrative in an effort to foster connection and rebuild trust with those closest to them. Understanding the difference between secrecy and privacy becomes essential in this process.

While secrecy is often rooted in fear and shame, leading to isolation and further pain, privacy is about selectively and intentionally sharing one's story with those who are deemed trustworthy and capable of handling it with respect. As clients navigate the delicate path of sharing their story with collateral partners, therapists play a crucial role in helping them discern when and how to transition from secrecy to privacy, ensuring that the sharing of their narrative strengthens connections rather than exposing them to further harm.

Secrecy often arises from a place of shame, fear, or the desire to avoid judgment or reprisal. Perpetrators of abuse frequently exploit secrecy as a weapon, using it to coerce their victims into silence and isolation. By manipulating the concept of secrecy, they create a shield behind which their harmful actions are hidden, perpetuating cycles of shame and suffering. In this way, secrecy becomes a tool of control, fostering an environment where the victim's voice is stifled, and their trauma is buried under layers of guilt and fear.

In contrast, privacy is about empowerment and the selective sharing of information with individuals who have earned trust. Privacy honors the client's autonomy and their right to control their own narrative. It acknowledges the importance of personal boundaries, allowing clients to decide who is worthy of bearing witness to their story. Privacy fosters trust and intimacy within relationships, as it is rooted in mutual respect and understanding rather than fear or shame.

The interplay between confidentiality, secrecy, privacy, and trust forms the foundation of the therapeutic alliance. In the context of relational trauma, where trust has often been shattered, and secrets have festered in darkness, confidentiality serves as a beacon of hope. It provides a safe space where healing can take root, free from the manipulative forces that once exploited secrecy. However, confidentiality must be wielded with wisdom and discernment. It is a double-edged sword—when used with care, it can protect and empower, but if misused, it can inadvertently reinforce the patterns of control and silence that the perpetrator once imposed.

The therapist's role in navigating these concepts is delicate and requires a deep commitment to the client's well-being. Not everyone is entitled to the honor of holding the client's story. The therapist must help the client discern who can be trusted with their narrative and who cannot. This discernment is essential, especially when dealing with the aftermath of relational trauma, where the misuse of confidentiality by perpetrators has caused significant harm.

In therapy, the goal is to move away from the secrecy that perpetuates suffering and toward the privacy that fosters healing. This process involves guiding the client to understand that while their story is precious and deserves to be protected, not everyone is entitled to know it. The therapist's task is to create an environment where the client feels safe enough to share, while also empowering them to maintain control over who has access to their narrative.

Ultimately, confidentiality, when practiced with integrity and empathy, becomes a powerful tool for healing. It allows the client to reclaim their story from the shadows of secrecy and shame, to share it with those who will honor it, and to rebuild trust in a world where it was once broken.

In some situations, a client may express a desire for their therapist to communicate with a collateral partner, such as a spouse or employer. This might involve sharing specific information about the client's progress or discussing ways in which the collateral partner can support the client's therapeutic goals. In these cases, it is crucial that the therapist obtains the client's informed consent before sharing any information. The client should be fully aware of what will be disclosed, to whom, and for what purpose. This consent should be documented, and the therapist should remain vigilant in ensuring that any disclosures are in line with what was agreed upon.

However, even with the client's consent, the therapist must be mindful of the potential impact of involving collateral partners. In some cases, sharing information with a collateral partner can inadvertently compromise the client's sense of safety or control. For example, if a client is in therapy to address issues related to an abusive relationship, involving the abusive partner in the therapeutic process can be extremely risky. The therapist must carefully assess the potential risks and benefits of involving collateral partners and should prioritize the client's safety and well-being in all decisions.

Confidentiality also becomes complex when dealing with clients who are mandated to attend therapy by an employer or legal system. In these situations, the therapist may be required to provide reports on the client's attendance, participation, or progress. However, even in these cases, the therapist must carefully navigate what information is shared and ensure that the client's confidentiality is protected as much as possible. The therapist should be clear with the client from the outset about what will be reported and should obtain the client's informed consent for any disclosures.

When clients feel ambivalent about how much to disclose to their collateral partners, such as a spouse or family member, it's crucial to explore the underlying function of the disclosure. At a certain stage in therapy, clients may feel a strong urge to disclose everything to their intimate partners as a form of confession, seeking relief from the burden of secrecy. While this can provide some short-term emotional relief, it often does not lead to the outcome the client expects and may result in misunderstandings or further disconnection.

The therapist's role is to help the client navigate and pace these disclosures, ensuring that the information shared effectively achieves their intended goals—whether that's building connection, seeking understanding, or addressing specific issues—while also considering the potential risks of misinterpretation or judgment. Pacing is essential, as it allows the client to disclose information in a way that is more likely to be interpreted as intended, fostering a positive impact on the relationship. By supporting the client in pacing their disclosures, therapists help ensure that communication strengthens the relationship rather than causing unintended harm. The therapist should respect the client's autonomy while guiding them to consider how the timing and content of their disclosures might impact their relationships in both positive and negative ways.

Moreover, confidentiality and safety are intertwined when working with clients who have experienced trauma, especially relational trauma. These clients may have learned to associate disclosure with danger, particularly if their trauma involved betrayal by someone they trusted. For these clients, the fear that their therapist might share their story with others can be a significant barrier to engagement in therapy. The therapist's ability to maintain confidentiality is not just about following ethical guidelines; it is about creating an environment where the client feels safe enough to explore their trauma without fear of further betrayal.

It is also important for therapists to be aware of how counter-transference might impact their handling of confidentiality when working with collateral partners. Countertransference refers to the therapist's emotional responses to the client, which can sometimes cloud their judgment. For example, if a therapist feels a strong sense of empathy for a client who is struggling in a relationship, they might be tempted to share more information with the collateral partner in an effort to help the client. However, this can compromise the client's confidentiality and may not be in their best interest.

To navigate these complexities, therapists must engage in regular self-reflection and supervision. By examining their own emotional responses and biases, therapists can ensure that they are upholding confidentiality and prioritizing the client's safety and well-being. Supervision provides an opportunity for therapists to discuss challenging cases and receive feedback on how to manage confidentiality in complex situations.

Ultimately, confidentiality is not just about keeping secrets; it is about creating a space where clients feel safe enough to explore their deepest wounds and fears. When collateral partners are involved, this task becomes more challenging, but it is no less important. Therapists must navigate the delicate balance between maintaining confidentiality and involving collateral partners in a way that supports the client's therapeutic goals. This requires a deep commitment to the client's safety, autonomy, and well-being.

In summary, confidentiality is a cornerstone of the therapeutic process, especially when working with clients who have experienced trauma. It provides the foundation for trust, enabling clients to share their stories without fear of betrayal. However, when collateral partners are involved, maintaining confidentiality becomes more complex. Therapists must navigate these challenges with care, ensuring that the client's safety and well-being remain the top priority. By upholding the principles of confidentiality and involving collateral partners in a thoughtful and ethical manner, therapists can support their clients in their journey toward healing and recovery.

Chapter 14

NAVIGATING RELATIONSHIPS: THE IMPORTANCE OF BOUNDARIES IN RECLAIMING CONTROL

In therapy, having good boundaries is essential for both the client and the therapist, particularly when working with trauma survivors. For trauma survivors, boundaries are often compromised by their past experiences, making it difficult to establish and maintain healthy relationships. A trauma survivor will evaluate the authenticity of the therapeutic relationship based on how well boundaries are maintained. Boundaries provide structure and clarity, allowing the survivor to understand the limits and expectations of the relationship, which fosters trust and safety. For instance, when a therapist informs a client that they will be unavailable for a period because they are going out of town, it signals respect for the client's emotional needs while acknowledging the therapist's limitations. This clear communication about emotional bandwidth is crucial in establishing a relationship where both parties feel understood and respected.

For trauma survivors, the concept of boundaries may feel foreign or unclear. Their experiences may have involved boundary violations, manipulation, or enmeshment, leading to confusion about what is acceptable in relationships. In therapy, boundaries serve as a tool for the survivor to learn how to engage in healthy interpersonal interactions. Good boundaries allow the client to feel safe, as they understand that the therapeutic relationship is predictable, respectful, and designed to honor their personal space, emotions, and needs. Through this experience, the trauma survivor begins to understand how to implement and maintain boundaries in their own life, fostering healthier relationships outside of therapy.

Therapists must be mindful of both external and internal boundaries in their work with trauma survivors. External boundaries are more obvious—such as respecting personal space or the time constraints of a session—but internal boundaries, including emotional and mental limits, are equally important. These internal boundaries are often tested when therapists engage deeply with their clients' trauma stories, which can lead to vicarious trauma or burnout if not carefully managed.

For our client John, external and internal boundaries are critical to understanding how his past trauma shapes his current behaviors and relationships. Externally, John struggles with boundaries in his professional life, where his hyperfixation on work allows him to maintain control and avoid vulnerability. His inability to set limits on his time and energy, often working late and overcommitting, is a reflection of how he uses work as a shield from emotional exposure in his personal life. This lack of external boundaries blurs the line between work and personal relationships, leading to strain, especially with his wife, who feels neglected.

Internally, John's boundaries are compromised by his emotional responses. He avoids confronting the deeper pain of his past abuse by compartmentalizing his emotions, relying on transactional relationships like those with sex workers to maintain a sense of control. His inability to set internal boundaries leads to emotional disconnection, making it difficult for him to engage authentically with his wife and others. This internal boundary issue manifests in his compulsive need for secrecy and avoidance of vulnerability, preventing him from being fully present in intimate relationships.

One of the significant challenges therapists face when working with trauma survivors, particularly survivors of interpersonal trauma, is the risk of secondary trauma, also known as vicarious trauma. Secondary trauma occurs when therapists absorb the emotional weight of their clients' experiences, leading to emotional distress, physical symptoms, and changes in worldview. This is especially common when therapists work with male survivors of trauma, as societal expectations surrounding masculinity and vulnerability can add layers of complexity to the therapeutic relationship.

A key phenomenon in secondary trauma is the parallel process. In a parallel process, the therapist unconsciously mirrors the emotional experiences of the client. For example, a therapist working with a male survivor of interpersonal trauma may start to feel overwhelmed by emotions such as anger, fear, or helplessness—emotions that mirror what the survivor is experiencing. This emotional mirroring can blur professional boundaries and impact the therapist's ability to provide effective care. If left unaddressed, it may lead to burnout or compassion fatigue, ultimately reducing the therapist's capacity to contain the client's trauma.

The parallel process is especially potent in cases involving trauma because of the depth of emotion and pain that clients bring to therapy. Therapists must be vigilant about maintaining their internal boundaries—recognizing their own emotional limits and seeking supervision when necessary. If a therapist feels overwhelmed by the intensity of their client's trauma, it is vital to take steps to manage this emotional response to avoid the negative consequences of secondary trauma.

Mirroring, although explored further later in the book, is important to emphasize here as it intersects with internal boundaries through the parallel process. Previously, we discussed how mirroring can dysregulate a client when unintentional or unconscious. However, when utilized with intention, mirroring can become a tool for regulation. A therapist can mirror a client's affect in a slightly upregulated way, allowing the client to feel seen and understood while also helping them regulate their emotional state within the relationship.

This intentional mirroring process is similar to how young children, who lack the cognitive skills to regulate their emotions, rely on co-regulation from caregivers. Over time, they internalize these skills. For survivors of interpersonal abuse, a similar dynamic occurs—except in abusive relationships, mirroring was often used as a tool for manipulation and control. In therapy, intentional and attuned mirroring helps undo the manipulative patterns of the past, fostering emotional safety and offering a path toward healthy self-regulation.

Countertransference refers to the emotional reactions a therapist has to a client's experiences, often stemming from the therapist's unresolved issues or biases. In cases of male survivors of trauma, countertransference can be particularly challenging. Therapists may experience feelings of inadequacy, powerlessness, or frustration when working with male survivors, especially if they hold subconscious beliefs about masculinity and vulnerability. For example, a therapist may feel uncomfortable if they believe that men are supposed to protect themselves or that expressing vulnerability is a weakness. These countertransference reactions can blur boundaries and compromise the therapist's ability to remain objective.

It is essential for therapists to recognize their own emotional responses and maintain clear boundaries to prevent countertransference from impacting the therapeutic relationship. This may involve engaging in personal therapy, supervision, or consultation to process these feelings and ensure that they do not interfere with the client's healing journey. Without this self-awareness, therapists may inadvertently reinforce harmful societal messages about masculinity or over-identify with their clients, leading to ineffective treatment.

To understand countertransference and transference, it's essential to grasp the concept of a trigger. A trigger occurs when our emotional response to a situation is disproportionate to the event at hand. Triggers are often rooted in past trauma, and when triggered, our brains respond as if the past event is happening in the present. One critical aspect of this is that the brain, when triggered, does not recognize the passage of time. This means we emotionally revert to how we felt during the original traumatic event, often as children, and we subconsciously believe that the limited resources we had at that time are still the ones we possess now.

This is where a fair witness in the therapeutic relationship becomes crucial. The therapist can help challenge the disproportionality of the response, providing a safe space to explore why the reaction feels so overwhelming and what part of the past is being reactivated. By recognizing the presence of the trigger and its root in unresolved trauma, the therapist can guide the client toward understanding that they have more resources now than they did at the time of the original trauma.

In John's case, he experiences a disproportionate emotional response when his wife makes decisions about their finances without consulting him. This often leads to intense feelings of anger and helplessness. His reaction, seemingly out of proportion to the financial decision, is rooted in past trauma—specifically, the powerlessness he felt as a child when his stepfather controlled the family finances and disregarded John's needs. When his wife makes decisions about money, John's brain interprets the situation as if he is once again that powerless child, unable to assert control. He responds as though he is reliving the trauma, believing that he still lacks the resources to deal with the situation effectively. In therapy, the role of the fair witness is to help John recognize the connection between this trigger and his past trauma, and to help him develop the awareness that he now has the ability and resources to approach the situation differently.

In the case of countertransference, therapists themselves can be triggered by their clients' stories or behaviors, leading to emotional reactions that are not in proportion to the current situation. This often occurs when a client's trauma resonates with the therapist's own unresolved issues. For example, if a therapist had personal experiences of financial insecurity growing up, they may find themselves feeling overly protective or defensive when working with John on his financial-related trauma. The therapist's strong emotional reaction could cloud their judgment and interfere with providing effective support to the client.

In these situations, it's crucial for therapists to recognize when countertransference is occurring and seek supervision or peer support. A supervisor or peer can act as a fair witness for the therapist, helping them identify and process their emotional response. By discussing the countertransference in supervision, the therapist can gain perspective on their reactions, manage them more effectively, and ensure that they are not projecting their own unresolved issues onto the client. This process not only protects the integrity of the therapeutic relationship but also helps the therapist maintain their emotional well-being, ensuring that they can continue to support their clients effectively.

PHYSICAL, EMOTIONAL, AND MENTAL BOUNDARIES IN THERAPY

There are three primary types of boundaries in therapy: physical, emotional, and mental. These boundaries play a crucial role in the therapeutic relationship, but they can become distorted or violated due to a client's experiences of trauma.

First, it is important for clients to be able to identify and understand the different types of boundaries in their lives—emotional, physical, and mental. These boundaries exist both externally, in relationships with others, and internally, in how we allow external situations to affect us. Trauma, however, distorts these boundaries, often leading individuals to either overly restrict themselves or allow too much intrusion into their personal space, emotions, or thoughts.

Second, as part of the healing process, it is essential for these boundaries to be re-established in clients' lives. Trauma can cause physical boundaries, for example, to become overly rigid, where a person avoids all physical contact, such as refusing a handshake or a hug, even when they may desire connection. Conversely, trauma can lead to porous boundaries, where individuals struggle to protect themselves, allowing others to invade their emotional or physical space too easily.

A good illustration of this distortion is seen in something as simple as greeting someone. Some trauma survivors may insist on minimal contact, such as a fist bump, to avoid any potential triggers, while others may feel compelled to accept a hug despite their discomfort. Re-establishing healthy boundaries—knowing when and how to set limits and when to allow closeness—becomes a key part of the recovery process, enabling clients to regain control over their personal space and emotional well-being without being governed by trauma responses.

Physical boundaries refer to personal space and touch. Clients who have experienced trauma, especially sexual trauma, may struggle with understanding what is permissible in terms of physical boundaries. For example, a survivor might misinterpret a gesture of care, like a hand on the shoulder, or might feel uncomfortable with closeness, even in non-threatening situations. Clarifying and reinforcing these boundaries is crucial for helping clients feel safe and empowered in their relationships.

Emotional boundaries involve how we feel and internalize our relationships. Many trauma survivors struggle to differentiate their own emotions from those of others, leading to enmeshment or emotional distancing. Enmeshment refers to the inability to separate one's emotions and needs from those of others, often resulting in over-involvement or over-identification with another person's feelings. This is a common coping mechanism for trauma survivors, especially those who learned to prioritize others' needs to maintain safety in abusive environments. In therapy, it is essential to help clients establish healthy emotional boundaries, so they can experience empathy and connection without becoming overwhelmed or losing themselves in the emotions of others.

An example of internal boundaries within a friendship can occur when a client feels compelled to "rescue" a friend who is consistently in need of help. For instance, if the friend is facing financial trouble, relationship issues, or emotional distress, the client may immediately jump in to solve the problem without pausing to assess their own capacity. The client may take on the friend's struggles as though they are their own, feeling responsible for fixing everything.

In this situation, the therapist's role is to help the client explore their role in the relationship and whether they are acting from a place of true capability or from a sense of obligation. The therapist can guide the client to first consider their own needs: Are they emotionally, physically, or financially capable of helping their friend at this moment? Or is the client stepping in because they feel that being a friend requires self-sacrifice, even at the expense of their own well-being? This performative element—the belief that they must give up their own needs to stay in the relationship—can be a key factor in why the client struggles with internal boundaries.

The therapist can also help the client reflect on the history of the friendship, asking important questions about equity: Has the friend been there for them in times of need, or is the relationship one-sided? Recognizing patterns of imbalance can provide insight into whether the client's caregiving is rooted in genuine desire or an unhealthy obligation to maintain the friendship by overextending themselves. This awareness allows the client to better understand their role, their boundaries, and how they can maintain relationships without sacrificing their own needs.

The fawn response is one common manifestation of poor emotional boundaries. This survival mechanism involves placating or appeasing others to avoid conflict or harm. Trauma survivors who adopt the fawn response may engage in people-pleasing behaviors as a way to maintain a sense of safety and connection, even at the expense of their well-being. Therapy provides an opportunity to recognize these patterns and begin building healthier emotional boundaries, where the client can balance their needs with those of others.

Mental boundaries refer to an individual's ability to maintain their thoughts, beliefs, and opinions without undue influence from others. For trauma survivors, especially those who have experienced gaslighting or manipulation, maintaining these boundaries can be particularly challenging. Gaslighting erodes a person's trust in their own perceptions of reality, leading to confusion, self-doubt, and a sense of helplessness. In therapy, clients often need support in recognizing and asserting their mental boundaries, learning to stand firm in their beliefs and values while still engaging in relationships with others.

This concept of mental boundaries intersects with the personality trait of open vs. closed-mindedness, as defined by the Big Five personality styles, that was addressed in earlier in the book. Individuals who score higher in openness tend to be more receptive to new ideas and willing to explore different perspectives, which can be a strength. However, in the context of trauma, particularly for survivors of manipulation, this openness can sometimes lead to an overreliance on others' opinions, leaving them vulnerable to having their thoughts or beliefs overridden. Survivors may struggle to discern their own views from those of others, making it hard to stand firm in their beliefs.

On the other hand, those who lean toward closed-mindedness tend to be more rigid in their thinking, often sticking to familiar beliefs and resisting new information. While this can sometimes serve as a protective mechanism for trauma survivors, helping them avoid further confusion or manipulation, it can also prevent growth and the integration of new, healthy perspectives in their healing process.

The therapist's role is to help the client find a balance between openness and closed-mindedness by strengthening mental boundaries. For the more open-minded client, this may involve learning when to trust their own instincts and avoid being overly influenced by others, especially in situations that could repeat patterns of gaslighting or manipulation. For the more closed-minded client, therapy might focus on creating space for healthy flexibility—encouraging them to open up to new ideas and trust their ability to evaluate and integrate these ideas without compromising their core values or beliefs. Ultimately, building mental boundaries helps trauma survivors regain control over their thoughts and engage in relationships from a place of strength and clarity.

Exploring these physical, emotional, and mental boundaries is critical for survivors of trauma. By understanding and reinforcing boundaries, therapists can help clients navigate their relationships more confidently and assertively. Additionally, addressing boundary issues within the therapeutic relationship itself provides valuable insight into the client's broader struggles with boundaries and helps them practice boundary-setting in a safe, controlled environment.

One important distinction that clients must learn in therapy is the difference between rules and boundaries, especially in the context of power dynamics. In abusive or controlling relationships, perpetrators often impose rules on their victims as a way to exert control. These rules blur the lines between acceptable behavior and personal boundaries, leaving survivors confused about their own autonomy and needs. Over time, victims may internalize these rules as if they were mutually agreed upon, even though they were imposed to maintain control. This dynamic can create confusion for survivors, making it difficult for them to recognize their own needs and maintain agency within relationships.

In John's case, his wife developed a rule that she would control all of his online activities, including monitoring his use of the internet, pornography, and social media. This rule was framed as necessary for the relationship's survival, as it was a response to John's inappropriate sexual activities, including solicitation and his use of pornography. The rule became an unspoken expectation—John felt that abiding by it was the only way to keep the relationship intact. Over time, he internalized this control as something essential to maintaining their marriage, even though it left him feeling trapped, without privacy, and disempowered.

In therapy, John began to explore the difference between this imposed rule and what a healthy boundary might look like. While the rule was focused on controlling his behavior to repair the damage done by his sexual activities, a boundary would have involved mutual agreement and respect for both partners' needs and autonomy. John realized that, instead of being a collaborative solution, the rule only deepened his sense of powerlessness and shame. He learned that boundaries are meant to protect personal space and freedom while still addressing the needs of the relationship, whereas the rule imposed by his wife served to control him and created a disproportionate power dynamic in their relationship. This awareness allowed John to begin reclaiming his autonomy and start setting healthier, more balanced boundaries within the relationship.In therapy, helping clients differentiate between rules imposed by others and their own boundaries is a critical part of the healing process. Therapists can help clients understand that boundaries are about self-management and protection, not about controlling others. This shift empowers clients to reclaim their autonomy and assert their boundaries in ways that feel safe and healthy. By focusing on how clients can manage their own responses to boundary violations, therapy helps individuals regain a sense of agency in their relationships.

Boundaries are essential for both clients and therapists in maintaining a healthy therapeutic relationship and fostering recovery from trauma. For therapists, setting clear external and internal boundaries protects against secondary trauma and ensures emotional well-being. For clients, learning to recognize and assert boundaries is critical in both therapy and their personal relationships.

The parallel process highlights how the boundary struggles of clients can mirror those of therapists, with clients testing boundaries to assess safety and therapists potentially overstepping in response. Recognizing the function of this behavior—often a reenactment of past relational patterns—helps both parties manage these dynamics effectively. Clients test boundaries to explore safety, and when therapists maintain clear boundaries, they provide a sense of security and trust.

Through this process, clients gain insight into how physical, emotional, and mental boundaries function, helping them build confidence in their relationships. By modeling healthy boundaries, therapists offer a roadmap for trauma survivors, enabling them to heal and create healthier connections.

Chapter 15:

THE POWER OF VULNERABILITY: HOW SELF-DISCLOSURE BUILDS TRUST

In the therapeutic process, particularly when working with male survivors of sexual trauma, the intersection of humility and therapist self-disclosure plays a crucial role. Self-disclosure, when used thoughtfully and strategically, can enhance connection, empathy, and trust within the therapeutic relationship. For vulnerable clients such as male survivors, who may struggle with issues of masculinity, vulnerability, and shame, the act of a therapist sharing personal experiences can humanize the therapist, reduce the inherent power differential in therapy, and create a more egalitarian dynamic. This shift allows the client to feel more understood and supported.

However, self-disclosure is a tool that must be used with precision and care. It is not simply about the therapist sharing their experiences; it's about choosing when and how to share, always with the goal of fostering connection and furthering the client's healing process. The therapist's narrative must never overshadow the client's. If self-disclosure is excessive or irrelevant, it risks shifting the focus away from the client's needs and experiences, potentially leading to disconnection, alienation, or even resentment. The client may feel that their story is being minimized or overshadowed, which can hinder the therapeutic process.

When addressing complex and sensitive issues like sexuality and trauma, self-disclosure becomes even more delicate. Male survivors of sexual trauma, in particular, may carry societal burdens related to masculinity, often making it difficult for them to express vulnerability or discuss their trauma openly. Here, the therapist's role in building a safe and empathetic environment is essential. By sharing carefully chosen personal experiences, the therapist can validate the client's feelings and normalize their struggles, thereby accelerating trust-building and creating an emotionally safe space for the client to explore their trauma.

However, the use of self-disclosure also increases the risk of countertransference—when the therapist's unresolved personal issues or biases begin to affect their perception and response to the client. This is particularly relevant when dealing with shared experiences, as the therapist might unintentionally project their own feelings onto the client. For instance, if the therapist has unresolved issues related to their own experiences with vulnerability or masculinity, this could subtly influence the therapeutic dynamic, creating challenges in maintaining the client's autonomy in the therapeutic space.

The risk of therapist self-disclosure is the potential for it to become a "shiny object" for the therapist—a distraction that feels like it's fostering connection but instead shifts the focus onto the therapist. When self-disclosure is used without careful reflection, it can unintentionally put the therapist at the center of the conversation, leaving the client feeling obligated to take care of the therapist emotionally. This role reversal can disrupt the therapeutic process and dilute the power of the client's narrative. Through reflective practice and supervision, therapists can sharpen their ability to recognize when self-disclosure truly serves the client's needs versus when it may be more about the therapist's desire to connect. Navigating the delicate boundary between self-disclosure and maintaining the client's focus requires constant self-awareness and a commitment to keeping the therapeutic space centered on the client's healing.

Supervision and peer consultation are vital tools for therapists navigating the fine line between beneficial self-disclosure and countertransference. Supervision allows therapists to reflect on their emotional reactions and ensures that their interventions remain dedicated on the client's needs, not their own. In this context, supervision serves as a "fair witness," helping therapists identify moments where their own narrative might be intruding on the client's journey. By recognizing and managing these reactions, therapists can uphold the integrity of the therapeutic process and keep the focus on the client's healing.

It is also essential to approach each client's narrative with humility. Even if a therapist shares common experiences with a client, they must always acknowledge that the client's journey is unique. No matter how similar the experiences may seem, the therapist's role is not to relate but to listen, validate, and support the client as they navigate their trauma. Therapists must be cautious not to assume they fully understand the client's experience, as this can lead to over-identification, come across as disingenuous, and minimize the client's individual narrative.

Self-disclosure can also be effectively used through a more subtle lens by framing it as a shared human experience. For example, a therapist might say, "Some people feel that way," or "Other clients have reported feeling this way," to help normalize the client's emotions or reactions. This approach can be particularly useful when a client is struggling with feelings of shame or isolation, especially in situations where society might view their response as unhealthy or unacceptable. By gently normalizing the experience, the therapist can help the client understand that their feelings and reactions are typical responses to difficult situations. This not only alleviates shame but also fosters a sense of connection and understanding, helping the client feel less alone in their struggles.

For male survivors of sexual trauma, these dynamics are especially important. Many men who have experienced sexual abuse may feel conflicted about discussing their trauma due to societal expectations around masculinity. Fears of being dominated, perceived as weak, or being sexualized in the therapeutic space can inhibit their willingness to share. A therapist's self-disclosure, when done thoughtfully, can bridge this gap, showing the client that it is possible to discuss difficult topics without judgment or fear. By modeling vulnerability and openness, the therapist helps the client feel safe enough to do the same.

Yet, the therapist must always be mindful of timing, quantity, and purpose when using self-disclosure. The goal should always be to serve the client's healing process. If used judiciously, self-disclosure can strengthen empathy and trust, creating a therapeutic environment where the client feels supported and understood. However, it must never overshadow the client's experiences or shift the focus away from the client's journey.

Highlighting the fact that the intersection of humility and therapist self-disclosure is a delicate but powerful tool in therapy, particularly when working with male survivors of sexual trauma. By using self-disclosure thoughtfully, with sensitivity and a focus on the client's needs, therapists can create a stronger therapeutic alliance, foster trust, and ultimately facilitate healing. It is through this balance of sharing and listening that therapists can help their clients move beyond their trauma and toward recovery.

FROM ACCOLADES TO AUTHENTICITY: JOHN'S JOURNEY THROUGH SELF-DISCLOSURE

John had spent most of his life performing, driven by a deep need to succeed. On the surface, he had everything anyone could ask for—a thriving business, financial security, and respect from his peers. His colleagues often praised his work ethic and sharp business acumen, holding him up as a model of success. Yet, despite these external accolades, John felt hollow inside. No matter how many awards he won or deals he closed, he couldn't shake the nagging feeling that something was fundamentally wrong with him. Beneath his polished exterior, John struggled with a pervasive sense of defectiveness that no amount of success could fix.

During one of our sessions, John confessed that no matter how much praise he received, it never felt like enough. "It's like I'm broken or something," he said, shaking his head. "I keep trying to prove myself, but no matter what I do, I still feel like I don't measure up."

It was a pivotal moment, and I felt it was the right time for careful self-disclosure. I said, "You know, I can really relate to what you're saying. I've been there myself—reaching what looks like success from the outside but still feeling like something's missing or that I'm not quite enough deep down. It's more common than you might think, especially when there's a disconnect between how others perceive you and how you see yourself."

John was silent for a moment, clearly absorbing the weight of my words. I could see a mix of relief and vulnerability in his eyes—

finally realizing he wasn't alone in feeling this way. My self-disclosure wasn't about me; it was to show John that this deep-seated fear of not being enough, which he believed could be his downfall, was a struggle others had faced too. It helped him understand that the incongruity between his external success and internal feelings of worthlessness wasn't unique to him, but something that many grapple with, often in silence.

As we continued our sessions, John began to uncover another painful truth: his relentless drive for success came at the cost of joy and connection in his personal life. He'd been so focused on performing and earning validation that he missed out on the simple pleasures of life—moments of joy with his children and intimacy with his wife.

"I can't tell you how many family dinners I've skipped because I was still working late, or how many times I've rushed through a conversation with my kids because I had a deal to close," John admitted, his voice heavy with regret. "I thought I was doing all of this for them, but now I realize that I've been using work to avoid feeling inadequate, and I missed out on them in the process."

John's performative nature—always chasing the next accomplishment, the next accolade—had created distance in his relationships. His wife, who had tried to connect with him emotionally, had become frustrated by his absence, both physically and emotionally. His children, too, had learned not to expect him at important milestones or even small moments of togetherness. John's success came with a heavy price—disconnection from the people he loved the most.

As we delved deeper, John began to understand that his drive wasn't just about achieving success for his family, as he'd often told himself. It was about trying to fill the void left by his deep-seated belief that he was defective. This need for external validation fueled his performative nature, pushing him to continually seek accolades in the hopes that one day, they'd make him feel whole. But those accolades were never enough, and in chasing them, he lost sight of the moments that could have brought him true fulfillment.

With clarity, John recognized that his success had become a mask for his feelings of inadequacy, rather than a reflection of his true desires or capabilities. He began to see that he had a choice. He could continue seeking external validation to cover up his feelings of defectiveness, or he could choose to perform on his own terms—without the need for others' approval—and reconnect with the joy he had lost.

Gradually, John's compulsion for success and external validation began to fade. Success still mattered to him, but now it was for his own sense of fulfillment, not to prove his worth to others. He started making decisions based on what was truly important to him, rather than the relentless drive to achieve. He began to prioritize his family, attending his children's games and sitting down for dinner, fully present, without the constant pull of work or the need to check his phone. With his wife, John started having deeper, more meaningful conversations, letting go of the pressure to appear perfect and instead embracing vulnerability. By releasing the need to achieve for the sake of others, John found himself more connected to what truly mattered in his life.

John had a powerful realization that the deep sense of defectiveness he carried wasn't something inherent in him—it had been imposed on him by his stepfather. He recognized that, as a child, the only way he could get attention from his stepfather was through performance. This began with the abusive dynamic, where he felt valued solely for being submissive and controllable, and later shifted to other areas like work and sports. As he excelled in sports, the same pattern reinforced itself—his achievements became the only way he felt worthy of attention. This ingrained in him the belief that "I'm not good enough, but what I do makes me loveable." John came to understand that his compulsion for success was tied to seeking love and validation through performance, a pattern rooted in the trauma of his past.

His business still thrived, but now it was driven by passion and choice—not by the need to fill the void of self-doubt. And most importantly, John rediscovered the joy and connection he had sacrificed for so long, understanding that accolades do not measure real success, but by the quality of the relationships and experiences that bring meaning to life.

Chapter 16

CURIOUS, NOT JUDGMENTAL: EMBRACING CURIOSITY IN THE HEALING PROCESS

Relational trauma often presents with layers of complexity, where emotions, behaviors, and reactions can seem contradictory and unclear. As therapists, we must adopt a stance of curiosity when engaging with the stories our clients bring into the therapeutic space. One of the greatest fears many trauma survivors face is being judged for the incongruencies between their feelings and how society perceives those feelings. This fear of judgment is particularly pronounced when survivors wrestle with emotions that don't fit neatly into societal expectations.

In response to the societal pressures and the internal conflict they experience, many survivors may outwardly project hatred toward their perpetrator, often as a defense mechanism. This projection can stem from how they see themselves today, from the perspective of an adult who understands the gravity of the abuse, and from the societal expectation that they should despise their abuser. The survivor may feel trapped by these conflicting emotions, leading them to believe that something is fundamentally wrong with them for having continued to return to the abusive relationship. They wonder, "If I went back, it must mean I'm defective in some way."

As therapists, it's crucial to approach this with curiosity rather than judgment. Instead of asking, "Why did you go back?"—which can feel accusatory and reinforce societal shame—we can reframe the question: "What do you think you were getting out of going back?" This shift in perspective opens up a space for the client to reflect on their past behaviors without the heavy burden of feeling that something is inherently wrong with them. It allows the survivor to explore the reasons they may have returned to the abuser, whether it was for attention, a sense of security, or some other emotional need. This curiosity-focused approach fosters self-compassion, giving the client the opportunity to understand that their behavior was not a reflection of personal failure but a response to their circumstances at the time.

In many cases, clients may come to the realization that, despite the abuse, there was something they craved from the relationship—perhaps the attention or validation the offender provided, even if it was toxic or harmful. When the therapist normalizes these feelings by saying something like, "Some clients have told me that they craved the attention their offender was giving them, and for them, the pay-off was worth it at the time," it helps the survivor feel less isolated in their experience. This validation removes the perception that their behavior was inherently defective and opens up space to reflect on their unmet needs.

Utilizing group work can be an essential goal in trauma recovery and is to provide a space where survivors can explore these dichotomous feelings—like loving and hating their abuser—in a collective setting. Group therapy offers a powerful platform for survivors to hear from others who have experienced similar emotional conflicts, helping them to realize they are not alone in their feelings. Often, a therapist's words of reassurance may not be enough to fully shift the survivor's perception of themselves. However, when other group members share their own struggles with the same conflicting emotions, it becomes easier for the survivor to challenge the belief that they are defective. Instead, they begin to see that their responses were a normal part of surviving trauma.

For many survivors, especially men, the secrecy surrounding their abuse creates an additional layer of shame and isolation. Society often perpetuates the idea that certain feelings—such as still caring for the abuser—are abnormal, making it difficult for men to admit their vulnerabilities. In group therapy, these barriers begin to break down. The shared experiences of others create a safe environment where survivors can confront and express emotions that they've kept hidden for so long. Group work validates that what society deems "abnormal" is actually a typical response for survivors, particularly in complex relational traumas. Through this collective exploration, survivors are empowered to challenge their internalized shame and gain new perspectives on their healing journey.

Through this process, the client can explore their current needs and how they might be different from those in the past. The goal is to help them understand that their actions, while possibly confusing or troubling in hindsight, were survival mechanisms at the time. They were trying to meet a need, and this insight can be incredibly powerful in reshaping how they view themselves. With this deeper understanding, the client can begin to explore what they need today—what healthy, fulfilling relationships might look like and how they can meet their emotional needs without resorting to past coping strategies.

By maintaining a stance of curiosity, the therapist helps the client reflect on their past and present behaviors without the suffocating weight of judgment. This approach allows for deeper exploration of the survivor's internal world, where shame can gradually be replaced with empathy and understanding for their younger self. Ultimately, this reflective process encourages healing, self-acceptance, and a more empowered understanding of their personal journey.

As therapists, when we remain curious about the client's experience, we offer a space where the survivor's feelings can be explored without fear of judgment. Instead of labeling these contradictory emotions as wrong or unhealthy, we ask questions like, "Why do you think you feel both love and hate?" or "What does it mean for you to have these feelings at the same time?" This encourages the client to explore their emotions, uncover their origins, and understand the complexity of trauma responses. Being curious allows the client to approach their own story with less judgment, creating an opportunity for greater self-compassion.

One of the most insidious aspects of trauma is that it doesn't recognize the concept of time. When we are triggered or reflect on the traumatic experience, it's as though we are transported back to that moment—believing that the emotions, power dynamics, and vulnerabilities we felt then are still true today. In those moments, we may feel powerless, as if we are still that version of ourselves, unable to act or change the situation. This belief in our continued powerlessness can lead to passivity, where doing nothing feels like the safest option because, in the past, avoidance may have been our only way to survive. Unfortunately, this passivity reinforces the idea that we deserve the bad things that happen to us, trapping us in a cycle of victimhood. Over time, this can result in avoiding difficult situations or emotions altogether, leaving us vulnerable to distraction by "shiny objects"—things that temporarily soothe or divert our attention but prevent us from addressing the real underlying issues. These distractions keep us stuck in avoidance, further perpetuating the belief that we are powerless to change our circumstances.

A powerful metaphor that illustrates the challenge of avoiding or suppressing thoughts and emotions is the "elephant in the room." If I ask you not to think about an elephant, chances are you'll immediately picture one, no matter how hard you try to avoid it, especially if one continues to talk about it. Similarly, the more clients attempt to suppress or control their thoughts—particularly those filled with judgment, shame, or confusion—the more persistent and overwhelming those thoughts become. Instead of trying to banish these unwanted feelings, the therapist encourages curiosity. What does the "elephant" represent or what is it´s function, how is it helpful for the client? What feelings or memories are surfacing that need attention? By embracing curiosity, the therapist and client can shift the focus from avoidance to exploration.

Curiosity also helps us examine our biases and how they influence our reactions. Imagine a situation where someone picks up your wallet after you drop it. Without curiosity, your initial reaction might be to assume that person is trying to steal it. This judgment shapes your response—anger, suspicion, maybe even confrontation. But if you approach the situation with curiosity, you might entertain the possibility that the person is trying to return your wallet to you. This curiosity opens up other potential explanations for their behavior and reduces the chances of misunderstanding.

The use of pacing is essential to cultivating curiosity, especially when working with trauma survivors. Our thoughts often serve the primary function of keeping us safe, prompting us to make quick decisions to avoid perceived danger. This rapid, reflexive response is rooted in survival instincts, where fast reactions can be lifesaving. However, when individuals have experienced trauma, their safety-seeking behaviors may look different than those of others, often shaped by the unique threats they've encountered. What once protected them in unsafe environments might now manifest as overreactions or reflexive behaviors that no longer serve them in their current lives.

Once a client can lean into their curiosity, they can start to recognize these patterns and understand that their current resources—emotional, psychological, and practical—are much stronger than they were during the traumatic event. When they truly believe that they have the tools today to keep themselves safe, they can begin to pace their responses, slowing down instead of immediately reacting to triggers. This process allows them to move away from old, reflexive behaviors that are based on outdated rules of survival and opens up the opportunity to identify possible distortions in their thinking.

Pacing enables clients to engage in a more deliberate reflection process, where they can pause and ask, "Is my response proportional to the situation? Am I interpreting this correctly, or is this based on an old fear?" This moment of curiosity shifts them from automatic, safety-seeking behaviors to a more thoughtful analysis of the current situation. They learn to ask the right questions, challenging their interpretations and exploring alternative ways of seeing and reacting.

In the parallel process, the therapist models this approach by slowing down in sessions and reflecting with curiosity instead of judgment. As the therapist paces the conversation, encouraging the client to explore their thoughts and emotions carefully, the client learns to adopt this pattern in their own life. This co-regulation helps clients understand that it is okay to take their time, to reflect before responding, and to trust that they now have the resources to handle the situation differently. Through this process, the client gradually learns to embrace curiosity, not as a luxury, but as a vital tool for safety and emotional well-being.

The same principle applies in therapy. Without curiosity, we may be quick to judge our clients' behaviors, labeling them as unhealthy or dysfunctional. But when we pause and ask why a behavior exists, what need it might be fulfilling, or what fear it might be protecting against, we create space for understanding. In trauma survivors, behaviors that seem counterintuitive—like maintaining an emotional bond with an abuser—often have deep roots in safety-seeking strategies. The survivor may have learned to stay connected to the abuser to reduce harm, even if that connection feels confusing or painful in the present.

As therapists, it's our role to embody Heinlein's concept of the "fair witness," an impartial observer who helps clients examine their thoughts and behaviors without bias. When a client shares an experience that feels contradictory or confusing, the therapist can introduce multiple interpretations of the data the client presents. By asking questions like, "What else could this behavior be telling us?" or "Could there be another explanation for why you feel this way?" the therapist helps the client see beyond their initial judgments and opens the door to curiosity.

One of the most challenging yet rewarding aspects of trauma work is helping clients move away from judgment toward curiosity. Judgment often stems from preconceived notions or societal expectations, creating a sense of inadequacy or guilt in the client. For example, a male survivor of sexual abuse might feel intense shame for not being able to "move on" or "get over it" as society expects. But instead of validating those societal judgments, the therapist invites curiosity: "Why do you think it's so difficult to let go of this?" or "What's happening in your body and mind when these feelings come up?" By fostering curiosity, the therapist helps the client explore their experience without the weight of societal expectations, leading to deeper understanding and healing.

This shift from judgment to curiosity not only helps clients understand their own behaviors and feelings but also improves their relationships with others. Often, trauma survivors struggle with trust, fearing that others will betray or abandon them. Encouraging curiosity allows them to challenge these fears without ignoring them. For example, a client might express distrust in a current relationship, saying, "I just know they're going to leave me." Instead of dismissing this belief, the therapist can ask, "What evidence do you have for this? What might be making you feel this way?" This helps the client differentiate between past trauma and present reality, encouraging them to engage more openly with their relationships.

At times, fostering curiosity requires the client to take a "leap of faith" by trusting that people can be trustworthy, even if past experiences suggest otherwise. This leap of faith involves stepping outside their comfort zone and testing the belief that others can be safe, supportive, and reliable. The therapist's role is to provide a non-judgmental, curious environment where clients can explore their doubts, take small steps toward trust, and gradually build confidence in their ability to navigate relationships. The goal is not to force trust but to invite the client to consider the possibility that trust is attainable and can lead to deeper, more fulfilling connections.

Curiosity also becomes a powerful tool in the therapeutic relationship itself. Clients may present their stories with incongruent data, or they may react in ways that seem disproportionate to the situation. Rather than jumping to conclusions, the therapist can explore these reactions, asking, "What does this response tell us about your experience?" or "Is there something missing that could explain this reaction?" By being curious rather than judgmental, the therapist creates a space where the client feels safe to explore even the most confusing or contradictory emotions.

Later in this book, we will explore the function of behavior in greater detail. By maintaining a curious stance, therapists can help clients move from judgment to exploration, allowing them to understand why they behave the way they do. This shift not only promotes healing but also empowers clients to make new choices based on self-compassion and awareness. Curiosity, when practiced consistently, fosters resilience, empathy, and ultimately a more profound sense of self-understanding and connection in relationships.

In essence, curiosity transforms the therapeutic process. It invites clients to explore their experiences without fear of judgment, opening the door to healing and growth. When therapists embody this approach, they empower clients to move beyond shame and confusion and toward a deeper, more compassionate understanding of themselves.

Chapter 17

UNDERSTANDING COPING MECHANISMS AND THE "SHINY OBJECT"

Coping mechanisms are strategies individuals employ to manage stress, regulate emotions, and navigate challenging situations. While some of these behaviors are often labeled as destructive by society, they serve important functions for those who use them, particularly trauma survivors. Instead of immediately judging or pathologizing these behaviors, it is crucial to understand their origins and how they function as responses to unresolved trauma. One such coping mechanism is what we refer to as the "shiny object"—a behavior that captures attention and provides short-term relief, often at the expense of long-term healing. Understanding the role of the shiny object within trauma recovery can help individuals move away from destructive patterns and toward healthier ways of coping.

Coping mechanisms, including shiny object behaviors, often develop as adaptive responses to stress or trauma. These strategies help regulate emotions, alleviate distress, and maintain psychological balance in environments where individuals feel unsafe or powerless. Over time, however, as their circumstances change, these once adaptive behaviors can become maladaptive, especially when they no longer serve their original purpose. For instance, a behavior that helped someone survive in a chaotic or abusive environment may become a barrier to healthy relationships or personal growth in safer, more stable settings.

ORIGINS OF THE SHINY OBJECT

The shiny object refers to behaviors that serve as distractions from emotional pain, intimacy, or other uncomfortable feelings that individuals are not yet ready to confront. These behaviors are often rooted in trauma and can become compulsive, acting as a form of avoidance. The shiny object is typically used to escape from the pain of past experiences, providing temporary relief while masking the deeper issues that need to be addressed for true healing to occur.

The shiny object is often tied to the core elements of PTSD: avoidance, anxiety, and compulsive repetition. In particular, these elements can manifest in interpersonal relationships, creating significant barriers to intimacy and connection. For example, anxiety might cause someone to become hypervigilant in relationships, making it difficult for them to trust their partner or feel secure. This hypervigilance can distort their perception of normal interactions, leading to unnecessary conflict or avoidance of deeper emotional connections. Avoidance, another key feature of PTSD, can lead to emotional detachment in relationships as individuals fear vulnerability, not wanting to feel taken advantage of again. Lastly, the compulsive repetition of behaviors—such as engaging in self-destructive habits like substance abuse or compulsive sexual behavior—can serve as an attempt to regain control over their bodies or experiences. These repetitive behaviors often recreate the conditions of past trauma, even if the individual is not consciously aware of it.

Over time, the shiny object becomes a tool for emotional survival. It allows individuals to cope with their trauma without having to confront it directly. However, this avoidance often perpetuates the cycle of pain, as the individual continues to use these behaviors to escape their emotions, preventing real healing from taking place.

UNDERSTANDING THE ADAPTIVE NATURE OF COPING MECHANISMS

It's essential to recognize that many coping mechanisms, including shiny object behaviors, start as adaptive responses to difficult or traumatic situations. For example, a child who experienced abuse may have learned to keep secrets or suppress their emotions to protect themselves from further harm. In the context of an abusive or neglectful environment, these behaviors serve as necessary survival tools. The problem arises when these behaviors continue into adulthood, where they become maladaptive in safer, more controlled environments.

In situations where individuals have greater autonomy or emotional support, the same coping mechanisms that once helped them survive may now hinder their ability to form healthy relationships or achieve personal growth. The behavior hasn't necessarily changed, but the context has. What was once a survival mechanism is now a barrier to intimacy and healing. This shift underscores the importance of understanding the function of these behaviors within the specific circumstances of the individual's life.

One example of this is the secrecy that often surrounds childhood sexual abuse. For a child, keeping the abuse secret may have been a way to maintain a sense of control or protect the abuser, who they might still feel attached to or dependent on for emotional validation. As adults, however, maintaining this secrecy can lead to continued feelings of shame, guilt, and confusion, particularly when the survivor attempts to form healthy, authentic relationships. The secrecy that once protected them now serves to reinforce the very trauma they are trying to escape.

THE ROLE OF AVOIDANCE, ANXIETY, AND REPETITION

The key elements of PTSD—avoidance, anxiety, and repetition—are integral to understanding shiny object behaviors. Avoidance allows the individual to sidestep emotional pain or vulnerability. For example, someone might engage in compulsive sexual behavior or substance use to avoid feeling the emotional weight of past trauma. Anxiety drives hypervigilance and fear in relationships, preventing the individual from trusting others or allowing themselves to be vulnerable. Repetition manifests in the compulsive nature of shiny object behaviors, such as repeatedly engaging in destructive actions even though they know it harms them or their relationships. These behaviors may temporarily offer relief, but they ultimately reinforce the trauma by keeping the individual stuck in a cycle of avoidance.

For instance, consider someone who engages in anonymous sexual encounters as a way to cope with unresolved trauma. The secrecy surrounding these encounters adds an element of danger or thrill, reinforcing the need to keep the behavior hidden. While this might provide temporary relief or distraction from underlying emotional pain, it further isolates the individual and perpetuates the cycle of shame and secrecy. The same can be said for individuals who seek out compulsive behaviors like substance abuse. In these cases, the shiny object—whether it's sex, drugs, or something else— becomes a focal point of avoidance, distracting the individual from the deeper emotional work they need to do.

UNDERSTANDING THE SHINY OBJECT
AS A DEFENSE MECHANISM

Society often labels these shiny object behaviors as pathological or destructive without fully understanding their origins. This can lead to further judgment, reinforcing the individual's sense of defectiveness or inadequacy. As a result, they may feel even more compelled to continue the behavior, believing that it is the only way to manage their pain. In therapy, it is important to help clients recognize that their shiny object behaviors, while destructive in the long term, were initially developed as survival strategies. They served a purpose—whether that was to numb emotional pain, avoid intimacy, or gain a sense of control.

The perceived destructiveness of the shiny object can itself become a shiny object that distracts from the real issues. Instead of focusing solely on the outward behaviors, therapists must guide clients in understanding the function of these behaviors and how they fit into the broader context of their trauma. By identifying the underlying emotions and needs that drive these behaviors, clients can begin to see that their coping mechanisms were not flaws but responses to overwhelming circumstances. This shift in understanding allows them to explore healthier ways of meeting those needs without resorting to self-destructive behaviors.

THE GIFT IN THE WOUND: TRANSFORMING
THE SHINY OBJECT INTO A SUPERPOWER

In trauma recovery, the concept of the "shiny object" is often seen as a distraction—something that pulls individuals away from the deeper emotional work that needs to be done. Whether it's compulsive behaviors, addictions, or other coping mechanisms, the shiny object serves as a means of avoiding pain, vulnerability, and difficult emotions. However, within this coping strategy lies an untapped strength, a "gift in the wound." The shiny object, while a form of avoidance, is also a defense mechanism that can, when understood and harnessed, become a tool of empowerment—a superpower that the individual can use consciously rather than reflexively.

The shiny object often emerges from a place of survival. It helps regulate overwhelming emotions, maintain control, or escape situations that once felt dangerous or unbearable. While these behaviors may seem destructive when overused, they are also evidence of the individual's resilience and resourcefulness. Recognizing the shiny object as a form of self-protection is the first step toward transforming it from a mere defense mechanism into something far more powerful.

To truly harness the shiny object as a superpower, the individual must first understand its original function. This requires a shift in perspective—from seeing it as a flaw or weakness to recognizing it as an adaptive response that served a purpose. In moments of trauma, the shiny object helped the individual cope with intense emotions, maintain psychological balance, and navigate overwhelming situations. It allowed for survival when other tools were unavailable.

For example, a person who turns to compulsive behaviors such as excessive work, substance use, or sexual activity may have developed these habits as ways to avoid emotional pain or gain a fleeting sense of control. The key is to acknowledge that these behaviors once provided relief and were a necessary means of navigating distressing situations. But as circumstances change, so must the role of the shiny object.

The ultimate goal in therapy is not to eliminate the shiny object but to refine its use. This involves helping the individual recognize when they are using it as a tool of avoidance and when it can be employed as a conscious coping skill. The shiny object, in its essence, represents a skill—a way of directing attention, managing emotions, and protecting oneself. It's a matter of learning when to engage it and when to choose other, healthier strategies.

For instance, the same drive that fuels compulsive behavior can be channeled into constructive outlets. Someone who has used workaholism to avoid emotions can learn to harness that focus and energy in more intentional ways, balancing it with self-awareness and emotional regulation. Similarly, an individual who engages in thrill-seeking behaviors to escape their past can learn to channel that risk-taking into positive challenges that promote growth and fulfillment.

The transformation occurs when the individual gains awareness of their shiny object and its triggers. Instead of reflexively using it to avoid emotional pain, they can consciously decide when and how to deploy it as a resource. Think of the shiny object like a volume dial on a stereo. Sometimes, the volume is turned up too loud, overwhelming everything else and drowning out the opportunity for deeper emotional processing. But the goal is not to mute it entirely; rather, it's to learn how to adjust the volume, so it plays at a level that complements life rather than controls it. This requires emotional intelligence and self-reflection, skills that can be cultivated in therapy through mindfulness, self-awareness, and intentional practice. By recognizing when the shiny object is too loud and turning it down to a manageable level, individuals can retain its benefits while avoiding its pitfalls. It's not about always using or avoiding it—it's about the degree to which it's used and finding the right balance.

For example, an individual might recognize that their shiny object behavior—such as the pursuit of high-intensity activities—is linked to their need for control and adrenaline. By understanding this, they can consciously choose to engage in those activities in a healthy way, such as pursuing challenging but constructive goals. Instead of avoiding vulnerability in relationships, they can balance their need for excitement with emotional intimacy, learning when to lean into connection and when to step back.

The key is learning how to navigate the space between avoidance and empowerment. In moments of overwhelm, the individual may still choose to engage their shiny object, but now they do so with awareness and intention. They recognize when they need to step back and self-soothe, but also when it's time to face the underlying emotions and heal. The shiny object becomes a tool in their emotional toolkit—used strategically, not out of habit.

For the individual, this shift offers the opportunity to reclaim agency over their emotional landscape. The shiny object no longer controls them; they control it. With this new perspective, what was once seen as a weakness or distraction becomes a strength. It enables them to navigate life's challenges with greater adaptability and self-compassion, knowing when to lean on their defense mechanisms and when to face the pain directly.

Transforming the shiny object into a superpower is about integrating the lessons learned from trauma with the capacity for growth. It's about teaching the individual that their ability to cope, once rooted in survival, can now be used to thrive. Through therapy, they gain the skills to distinguish between avoidance and empowerment, to deploy their shiny object with purpose and intention, and to live a life that is aligned with their values and desires.

Ultimately, the gift in the wound is the individual's ability to navigate both the shadows of their trauma and the light of their healing. The shiny object, once understood and harnessed, becomes a symbol of their resilience, a tool they can wield in their journey toward wholeness. By recognizing its function and learning how to use it wisely, the individual gains not just relief, but empowerment—the ability to live a life that is no longer defined by avoidance, but by choice.

THE ROLE OF THE FAIR WITNESS IN ADDRESSING SHINY OBJECT BEHAVIORS

A key concept in working with trauma survivors is the role of the fair witness—the therapist who remains nonjudgmental and curious about the client's behavior rather than immediately labeling it as destructive. By recognizing the function of the shiny object and validating its origin, the therapist helps the client understand that they were using this behavior as a way to survive. From there, the focus shifts to exploring healthier coping strategies that can meet the same emotional needs without causing harm.

In our society, behaviors like substance use, pornography consumption, people-pleasing, and excessive work or sports performance are often labeled as destructive, especially when they become problematic. The typical response is to tell the individual to simply "stop" the behavior. While some people can indeed quit these behaviors and move on without further consequences, many others struggle to stop despite significant negative outcomes. This struggle is often misunderstood and judged harshly by society.

Some see it as a sign of weakness or lack of willpower, while others believe the individual hasn't faced a significant enough consequence to quit, assuming they need to "hit rock bottom" first.

The perspective offered here challenges those common misconceptions. These behaviors—whether it's substance use, excessive work, or other shiny objects—serve a function for the individual. They are coping mechanisms that, for better or worse, help the person manage pain, anxiety, or unresolved trauma. For the individual, the relief these behaviors provide often outweighs the consequences, and this is where the complexity of addiction lies.

To better understand this, think about the tragic example of individuals trapped in the Twin Towers on 9/11. Many people, facing the impossible choice between burning in the fire or jumping from the building, chose to jump. From their perspective, they were going to die either way, but jumping offered them some control over how it happened. Similarly, for trauma survivors, the shiny object provides a form of control or relief, even if it ultimately leads to more harm. The "demons" of trauma are often invisible, lodged deep within the mind. For many, the shiny object offers temporary relief from these demons, which feels better than facing the overwhelming emotions head-on. The perception of the trauma survivor may be that stopping the behavior means facing unbearable pain.

Through a curious lens, we can begin to see that the problem isn't just the shiny object itself. The issue lies deeper, in the trauma and emotional pain that drives the behavior. Simply stopping the shiny object won't resolve the underlying problem. One of the core components of the addiction model in our society is the 12-step approach, which emphasizes abstinence from the substance or behavior as well as recovery through community. When we examine shiny object behaviors through the lens of both addiction and PTSD, we can see that these behaviors serve key functions: they provide temporary relief from emotional dysregulation, offer a sense of connection (even if superficial), and may be part of a compulsive cycle rooted in trauma.

For trauma survivors, especially men, the shame and fear of being seen as defective often contribute to these behaviors. Many think, "If people truly knew me, they wouldn't like me." This belief fuels avoidance—not just of difficult emotions but also of intimacy and connection. The behavior serves as a buffer, allowing the individual to avoid the vulnerability that comes with showing their true self. Additionally, there is often a compulsion to repeat the behavior, whether it's substance use or compulsive sexual activity, because the individual has tied their sense of self-worth or control to these actions.

In some cases, substances are directly linked to sexual experiences. For instance, some offenders will use substances to lower the defense mechanisms of their victims, leading survivors to believe that in order to engage in sexual activity, they must be high. This creates a dangerous association between substances and intimacy, making it even harder for the survivor to break the cycle of compulsive behavior. For men in the LGBTQ+ community, these challenges can be even more complex. The layers of trauma, social stigma, and rejection compound the emotional pain, making the shiny object—whether drugs, sex, or other behaviors—a powerful coping tool.

LGBTQ+ individuals often face additional trauma related to their identity, especially if they were excommunicated or rejected by their families. This rejection leaves them vulnerable, and they may seek acceptance and belonging elsewhere. For example, the use of substances like crystal meth within some gay communities is both a coping mechanism for the pain of rejection and a means of finding temporary connection. While the substance may offer momentary relief and a sense of community, it ultimately exacerbates trauma symptoms and leads to further isolation.

This complex intersection of trauma, substance use, and sexuality is common among survivors, particularly within the LGBTQ+ community. In these situations, the shiny object often provides temporary comfort in the form of connection, validation, or control—things that feel absent in other areas of the individual's life. But as the consequences of the behavior mount, the individual is left trapped in a cycle of shame, isolation, and compulsive repetition.

Repetition compulsion, a well-known concept in trauma theory, refers to the unconscious drive to repeat behaviors or re-enact scenarios that mirror the original trauma. This is often seen in sexual behaviors, where survivors of sexual abuse may become more sexually active as a way to reclaim control or normalize their sexual experiences. For many men who have experienced sexual abuse, this repetition becomes a means of coping with their feelings of defectiveness. They may believe that their increased sexual activity is a result of the abuse, which only reinforces their belief that something is inherently wrong with them.

The high rate of sexual abuse among men who have sex with men (MSM) adds another layer of complexity to this issue. Many MSM report being sexually abused, often at a higher rate than the general population. This increased vulnerability, combined with social stigma and rejection, contributes to the intricate relationship between trauma and sexual behavior in this community. For many, the compulsive nature of their sexual behavior is an attempt to regain control, but it often perpetuates the trauma instead.

The traditional addiction model focuses on stopping the behavior, but simply quitting the shiny object won't resolve the deeper issues at play. The behavior serves a function, and until that function is addressed, the individual will continue to struggle. The primary function of shiny object behaviors for trauma survivors is to provide relief from overwhelming emotions and a sense of connection, even if it's temporary. Understanding this allows us to approach the behavior with curiosity rather than judgment.

In therapy, the role of the fair witness is crucial in helping individuals explore the function of their shiny object behaviors. Instead of labeling the behavior as inherently bad or wrong, the therapist helps the client understand what the behavior is doing for them and why it feels necessary. This nonjudgmental curiosity allows the client to examine their coping mechanisms without shame and opens the door to exploring healthier alternatives.

One of the key components of recovery, particularly in the 12-step model, is community. For many individuals, substance use or other shiny object behaviors provide a form of connection, even if it is surface-level or destructive. For example, people who drink at bars or use drugs with others may feel a sense of belonging in those moments, even though the connection is through the substance rather than genuine intimacy. For trauma survivors, who often feel defective or unworthy of love, these shallow connections may feel like the best they can achieve. They avoid deeper connections out of fear of rejection, believing that if people really knew them, they wouldn't want to be close.

The function of the shiny object in this context is not just about numbing pain or avoiding emotions; it's about finding connection and validation. In therapy, it's essential to explore this need and help the client develop healthier ways of connecting with others.

The compulsion to engage in these behaviors stems not from a moral failing but from a deep-seated need for connection and relief.

Shiny objects can also serve as a way to maintain control. For some individuals, particularly those who engage in compulsive sexual behaviors, the element of control is central to their coping mechanism. They may choose to engage with sex workers or consume pornography to control the terms of the sexual encounter—whether it's dictating the timing, the positions, or the roles within the experience. This need for control often stems from a history of powerlessness, particularly for trauma survivors, and the behavior serves as an attempt to reclaim some sense of agency over their bodies and experiences.

To move beyond shiny object behaviors, individuals need to address the underlying trauma and emotional pain that drives their actions. This requires developing healthier coping mechanisms to replace the shiny object and building supportive, authentic relationships. The key to lasting recovery is not just abstaining from the behavior but understanding the function it served and finding new ways to meet those emotional needs.

In conclusion, shiny object behaviors—whether substance use, pornography, or excessive performance in work or sports—are often misunderstood in our society. While they can be destructive, they serve important functions for trauma survivors, helping them cope with emotional pain, avoid vulnerability, or find a sense of connection. Rather than focusing solely on stopping the behavior, it's essential to approach these behaviors with curiosity, understanding their purpose, and helping individuals develop healthier ways of addressing their needs. Through this compassionate lens, recovery becomes more about healing the underlying trauma than simply eliminating the symptom.

GROUP THERAPY AND THE IMPORTANCE OF SHARED EXPERIENCE

Group therapy can be a powerful tool for trauma survivors struggling with shiny object behaviors. In group work, clients have the opportunity to hear from others who have experienced similar feelings and behaviors, which helps reduce the sense of shame and isolation. Often, a therapist's validation alone is not enough to shift the client's perspective. However, when they hear other group members share the same struggles, it becomes easier to challenge the belief that something is wrong with them.

For many survivors, particularly men, the secrecy surrounding their trauma creates additional barriers to healing. Society often expects men to be stoic and self-reliant, which can make it difficult for them to admit to feelings of vulnerability or emotional pain. In a group setting, these barriers begin to break down. Survivors can explore the conflicting emotions they experience, such as feeling both love and hate for their abuser, and understand that these feelings are normal responses to trauma. Group therapy validates their experiences and provides a safe space for exploring emotions that they might otherwise hide out of fear of judgment.

When managing a male survivors' group, it is essential to establish clear guardrails that create a safe, non-judgmental environment where healing can take place. Male survivors often carry deep-seated fears of being judged or rejected, which can hinder their ability to open up and fully engage in the healing process. The group must function as a safe container that encourages vulnerability, trust, and connection while adhering to a set of principles designed to protect and empower the participants.

The first and most fundamental rule of the group is confidentiality. This extends beyond simply keeping the details of the group private from outsiders—it includes confidentiality among group members themselves. In any group, natural hierarchies may develop, and confidentiality ensures that any power dynamics cannot be misused to control or marginalize others within the group system. Confidentiality fosters a sense of safety, where each participant can trust that their personal experiences and disclosures will not be used against them or gossiped about by others in the group.

Another critical principle is creating a judgment-free zone, where men can share their thoughts, feelings, and experiences without fear of being criticized or perceived as "less than" by others. In a group setting, there is always a risk that members may feel judged as they judge themselves for their behaviors, coping mechanisms, or personal histories, particularly when these involve sensitive topics like sexual trauma. It is essential that the facilitator actively monitors how statements are made and intervenes when necessary to ensure that no one feels attacked or judged. This involves correcting responses that may come across as judgmental before they have a chance to escalate or damage the group dynamic.

One of the most effective ways to maintain a non-judgmental atmosphere in a group setting is to frame suggestions and feedback by focusing on personal experiences rather than offering advice or directives. For example, group members might say, "How I handled a similar situation was..." or "What resonates with me in your story is..." This approach encourages members to reflect on their own journeys, sharing how they've navigated challenges in a way that feels collaborative rather than prescriptive. By discussing their personal stories and strategies, participants can avoid creating a power hierarchy, ensuring that no one feels more "defective" than others. It also promotes a sense of shared experience and mutual understanding, deepening the feeling of community and fostering support among all group members. This way, feedback is shared respectfully and with empathy, allowing everyone to learn and grow from each other's experiences without feeling judged or inferior.

A critical element of the group's success is also teaching the principles of trauma recovery, specifically helping members understand how trauma affects the nervous system. Many survivors may be unaware of the physiological impact of trauma, such as the heightened fight-or-flight response or the ways in which trauma can distort their perception of safety and threat. Educating the group about the nervous system's role in trauma responses can demystify the overwhelming feelings they experience and reduce shame by helping them recognize that their reactions are normal, trauma-driven responses.

Another productive aspect of group work is recognizing and addressing the "shiny objects" in participants' lives—the coping behaviors that may seem destructive but serve a function. By helping men in the group identify their shiny objects and approach them with curiosity rather than judgment, the group can collectively explore healthier ways to meet their needs. For example, if a participant's shiny object is overworking or substance use, the group can gently help them explore the underlying need for control, connection, or escape that drives these behaviors. Then, together, they can brainstorm replacement behaviors that can fulfill those needs in a healthier, more sustainable way.

Education about trauma within a group environment is a vital component of the healing process for male survivors. Understanding how trauma affects the brain and body can demystify the overwhelming emotions and reactions that survivors often experience, reducing the shame and self-blame they may carry. By learning about the physiological responses to trauma—such as the fight-or-flight response, hypervigilance, emotional numbness, or dissociation—group members can begin to understand that their behaviors and reactions are not personal failures but natural, survival-oriented responses to past harm. This shared knowledge not only normalizes their experiences but also empowers them to take steps toward healing by recognizing when they are triggered and applying coping strategies in real-time. The group environment allows for open discussion, where participants can ask questions, share insights, and reflect on how trauma manifests in their daily lives, fostering a collective understanding and reinforcing the sense that they are not alone in their struggles.

Lastly, the combination of these elements—confidentiality, non-judgment, shared personal experiences, trauma education, and exploring the shiny objects—within the sacred space of the group setting creates a powerful catalyst for change. This sense of community and collective healing is often very difficult to replicate in individual therapy sessions. The group environment allows for vulnerability to be mirrored and validated by others, creating a unique sense of solidarity and support. In this way, group work can offer a transformative experience, where participants can challenge their long-held beliefs about themselves, build trust, and move forward in their healing journey.

By maintaining these guardrails and principles, the male survivors' group becomes a safe and powerful space for transformation, offering a deeper level of healing than might be possible in isolation. The support of the group helps each man move from a place of fear and shame to one of connection, resilience, and growth.

MITIGATING SHINY OBJECT BEHAVIORS

The first step in mitigating shiny object behaviors is understanding their function. Once clients understand that these behaviors served a purpose—whether it was to numb emotional pain, avoid intimacy, or gain a sense of control—they can begin to explore healthier ways of addressing their needs. This process requires trust in the therapeutic relationship. If clients don't trust their therapist or feel safe in the relationship, they will struggle to take the leap of faith required to change their behavior. Building trust through nonjudgmental curiosity and validating the client's experiences is key to this process.

Once trust is established, therapists can begin to challenge the core beliefs that drive shiny object behaviors. For example, a client might believe that they are unlovable or defective and that their behaviors are proof of this. By exploring these beliefs and offering alternative perspectives, therapists can help clients shift their thinking and move toward healthier ways of coping.

The ultimate goal is to replace shiny object behaviors with healthier strategies for meeting emotional needs. This might involve helping clients identify what they are truly seeking—whether it's connection, validation, or emotional safety—and finding ways to achieve those goals without resorting to self-destructive behaviors. For instance, if the client's shiny object is substance use, they might explore building more supportive relationships or engaging in activities that bring them joy and fulfillment.

The shiny object is a powerful coping mechanism rooted in trauma and avoidance. While these behaviors may appear destructive on the surface, they serve important functions for those who use them. By adopting a fair witness perspective and exploring the origins and functions of shiny object behaviors, therapists can help clients move away from judgment and toward curiosity. This approach opens the door to deeper understanding and healing, allowing clients to replace self-destructive behaviors with healthier coping strategies that promote long-term well-being. Through this process, survivors of trauma can learn to navigate their emotions, develop resilience, and build healthier relationships with themselves and others.

FROM SILENCE TO SUPPORT: JOHN'S ROLE IN COLLECTIVE HEALING

John had been attending group therapy for a few months, though at first, his participation was minimal. He would sit quietly, observing the other men in the room as they shared their stories of trauma, shame, and secrecy. The group was filled with men like him—survivors of interpersonal sexual trauma—many of whom carried the same burdens John had: the secret use of sex workers, the compulsive behaviors they couldn't seem to stop, and the sense of isolation that followed them wherever they went. Yet, despite hearing familiar echoes in their stories, John struggled to open up. He wasn't ready to own his narrative or confront the shame that had been weighing him down for so long.

John would report in individual therapy that he felt like an outsider in the group. His long-term marriage and successful business career seemed to set him apart from the other men, feeding into a belief that he was somehow different or perhaps even "better off" despite his trauma. This perception became a barrier to vulnerability, reinforcing his fear of opening up and sharing his experiences with the group. He worried that his achievements might make the others see him as less deserving of support, or that revealing the truth behind his success—how it masked deep pain and compulsive behaviors—would shatter the carefully constructed image he'd built. This fear perpetuated his disconnection, leaving him isolated in a room full of men who shared similar struggles but, in his mind, remained worlds apart from his own.

For months, John held back, feeling like an outsider even among these men who shared his experiences. His shame ran deep—he had kept his trauma a secret from everyone, even those closest to him. He feared that if people knew, they would see him differently, judge him, or think less of him. The group, though, became a safe space where, over time, he began to recognize a different truth: that the other men weren't judging him, just as they weren't judging each other. They were just trying to heal, like he was.

One night, a turning point came for John. A fellow group member shared his story, detailing how he had hidden his use of sex workers for years, ashamed of the compulsions he couldn't control. He spoke about the shame of keeping it from his wife, the guilt of hiding behind a facade, and the fear that he would never be free of the behavior. As John listened, something clicked. This man wasn't just telling his story; he was telling John's story too. The similarities were undeniable, and for the first time, John felt an intense urge to speak with authenticity.

When it was his turn, John hesitated, but the group had created an environment of curiosity, not judgment. With a deep breath, he shared his secret—the years of using sex workers to numb the pain, the way he'd hidden it from his wife, and the overwhelming shame that consumed him every day. As the words tumbled out, John was surprised by the group's response. There was no judgment, no recoiling in disgust, just understanding nods and quiet validation.

Others had been there too. Others had survived the same kind of trauma and responded with the same behaviors. His shame began to lighten as he realized that he was not alone.

Over the next few weeks, John found himself opening up more in group, sharing details about his trauma that he had never told anyone before. With each session, he learned more about how his past shaped his behavior, and the therapeutic relationship with his therapist was now complemented by the connections he was making with other men in the group. It allowed him to see beyond the one-on-one dynamic, anchoring him in the reality that healing was possible not just with a therapist but with other men, through shared vulnerability.

Through group participation, John learned that the secrecy surrounding his trauma had been its own prison, and sharing it was the key to his freedom. He began to make meaning of his reactions—his compulsions, his avoidance of intimacy, and the walls he had built to protect himself. The group became a place where he could test out new ways of coping with his triggers, flexing new emotional muscles that allowed him to navigate difficult situations with more clarity and confidence. Each time he shared, he chipped away at the belief that he was defective, and each time the group responded with understanding, he felt a little bit more healed.

The most significant shift came when John realized that his participation in the group wasn't just about him anymore. It was about the collective healing that happens when men, who are often taught to hide their vulnerabilities, come together to share their pain. He began to support other group members, offering his insights and experiences in a way that was both genuine and empathetic. The once passive observer was now an active participant in his own recovery and in the recovery of others.

As John grew more comfortable in the group, he noticed changes in his relationships outside of therapy. He began to connect more deeply with his wife and children, having honest conversations he never thought possible. The tools he learned in the group—the ability to recognize his triggers, to be curious rather than judgmental about his reactions, and to express vulnerability—became the foundation of healthier, more meaningful relationships.

Group therapy had given John something he never thought he'd find: hope. The shiny object of sex addiction had been the focus when he first entered therapy, but now, as he looked back, he could see that it was never about the behavior itself. It was about the pain underneath it, the unresolved trauma, and the unspoken shame that had shaped his life for so long. By owning his story and sharing it with others, John began to heal, not just from the trauma but from the belief that he had to face it alone.

Chapter 18

MODELING HUMILITY: THE THERAPIST'S ROLE IN FOSTERING TRUST AND CONNECTION

Humility is an essential aspect of the therapeutic process, particularly when working with trauma survivors, as it provides a foundation of trust and equity in the relationship. For male survivors of sexual trauma, humility from the therapist's side can feel like a profound equalizer. Often, these men have spent years feeling as though they have been controlled, manipulated, or belittled. The fear of vulnerability is heightened, as many survivors have lived in constant defense, trying to protect themselves from further harm. In this context, humility on the part of the therapist can serve as a key to unlock deeper trust and openness within the therapeutic space.

For trauma survivors, humility is not just about acknowledging personal weaknesses or mistakes. It is also about understanding the power dynamics that have long impacted their sense of self-worth. Many survivors, especially men, are afraid to be controlled again, and they may view vulnerability as a weakness rather than a strength. When a therapist shows humility by openly admitting errors or limitations in their practice, it creates a sense of equity, signaling to the client that this is a partnership, not a hierarchy. The therapeutic relationship thus becomes a space where the client can begin to drop their defenses and engage more fully with the healing process.

Humility encompasses both intrapersonal and interpersonal aspects. Intrapersonal humility means having an accurate and balanced view of oneself, recognizing both strengths and limitations without overestimating or underestimating one's worth. In therapy, this self-awareness allows the therapist to model a grounded sense of self-acceptance, encouraging clients to explore their own feelings of inadequacy or excessive self-criticism. When a therapist embodies intrapersonal humility, it signals to the client that it is okay to be imperfect—that mistakes, struggles, and vulnerabilities are part of the human experience, not evidence of defectiveness.

Interpersonal humility is equally critical. It refers to how one interacts with others, particularly in avoiding self-promotion or dominance in relationships. For male survivors of trauma, who may have had their sense of autonomy and control stripped away during their experiences, seeing humility in their therapist can be an empowering reminder that their voice matters. The therapist's openness and respect foster an atmosphere where the client feels safe to explore difficult emotions and share their narrative without fear of judgment.

The traditional addiction model often reinforces the idea that individuals battling addiction are inherently flawed or defective, leading to feelings of shame and isolation. It promotes the belief that recovery requires strict adherence to its framework, and any deviation is seen as failure, letting the addiction "win." This dynamic can create an imbalance of power, leaving the individual feeling powerless and reinforcing a sense of inadequacy. In contrast, a therapeutic relationship built on humility and equity shifts the focus. Instead of imposing authority, the therapist approaches with curiosity, exploring the deeper function of the behavior. This approach recognizes that the addiction may serve as a coping mechanism rather than a moral failing. Through this collaborative lens, the therapist and client can uncover the needs driving the addiction, allowing for self-awareness, healing, and growth, free from the oppressive idea of submission to the addiction model.

Humility also paves the way for curiosity within the therapeutic space. Trauma survivors often carry the heavy burden of judgment—both self-imposed and from society. They may believe that their responses to trauma, like hypersexuality or substance abuse, are personal failures rather than mechanisms of survival. The "shiny object," such as John's sex addiction, becomes the target of judgment, diverting attention from the underlying trauma and emotional pain driving the behavior. By fostering a non-judgmental, humble space, therapists can help clients move beyond superficial labels and begin to explore the root causes of their behaviors. This shift in focus from judgment to curiosity enables deeper healing and understanding, moving beyond the behaviors to address the trauma at their core.

The parallel process in therapy—where the therapist's behavior models for the client how to engage in their own self-exploration—is particularly important here. When a therapist practices humility by owning their mistakes or misjudgments, they demonstrate that vulnerability is a source of strength rather than weakness. For clients like John, who fear that revealing their imperfections will lead to further judgment or rejection, seeing the therapist embrace their own humanity can be transformative. It encourages the client to take similar risks in acknowledging their own behaviors without fear of losing the therapist's respect or care.

Self-disclosure from the therapist, when done carefully and with intention, is another aspect of humility that can support the healing process. For male survivors of sexual trauma, the dynamics of vulnerability and power can be particularly fraught. Many men in these situations have learned to equate vulnerability with weakness or danger, often due to societal expectations around masculinity. By judiciously sharing their own experiences or struggles—without overshadowing the client's journey—the therapist can humanize the relationship, reducing the power differential that often exists in therapy.

However, self-disclosure must be handled with care. The therapist's goal should never be to shift focus onto their own story but to create a bridge of empathy that makes the client feel seen and understood. In John's case, for example, his therapist might share how other clients have struggled with the shame of secret behaviors, like using sex workers, and how those behaviors were coping mechanisms tied to unresolved trauma. This kind of disclosure normalizes John's experience without minimizing his individual pain, allowing him to feel less isolated in his shame.

The role of humility in the therapeutic process is also about the therapist's willingness to seek feedback and recognize when they might need to adjust their approach. Supervision and peer consultation are vital tools in maintaining this humility, as they provide a space for therapists to reflect on their work, address countertransference, and ensure they remain client-centered. For male survivors, who may be highly sensitive to power imbalances due to their trauma history, knowing that their therapist is committed to their growth and willing to admit when they have made mistakes can further solidify trust.

Moreover, humility in therapy fosters curiosity—both in the therapist and the client. Curiosity becomes the antidote to judgment, inviting clients to explore their behaviors and emotions with openness rather than shame. For survivors of trauma, the compulsive repetition of certain behaviors, like hypersexuality, often serves a deeper function than is immediately apparent. Rather than rushing to pathologize or eliminate these behaviors, a curious, humble approach asks: "What purpose is this behavior serving? How does it help you cope with the pain you carry?" By shifting the focus from the "shiny object" to the underlying wounds, therapists can help clients like John uncover the true roots of their actions and begin to address them at their core.

Ultimately, humility in therapy is about creating a partnership where both therapist and client are engaged in the process of healing with openness and authenticity. For male survivors of trauma, who may have spent years feeling isolated, defective, or unworthy of care, this kind of relationship can be life-changing. It allows them to move beyond the shiny object that brought them into therapy and begin to explore the deeper layers of their pain with compassion, curiosity, and the understanding that vulnerability is not a weakness but a path to true healing.

Chapter 19

CHALLENGING BELIEFS WITH COMPASSION: NAVIGATING TRAUMA AND AUTHORITY BIAS

Trauma, especially when it occurs within interpersonal relationships, can profoundly distort an individual's perception of themselves and the world. These distortions, rooted in painful experiences, shape beliefs that often serve as barriers to healing. Trauma, in particular, sneaks into the mind and embeds itself into the fabric of one's belief system, fostering feelings of shame, guilt, and inadequacy. For many survivors, the belief that they are "damaged goods" or unworthy of love becomes deeply ingrained. These beliefs, shaped by authority bias, are further reinforced by the narratives of their abusers, making it difficult for survivors to recognize their inherent worth.

Authority bias is the tendency to attribute greater accuracy and trustworthiness to the opinions, beliefs, or instructions of figures we perceive as authoritative, regardless of whether those views are valid. In the context of trauma, especially interpersonal sexual trauma, this bias often begins with our primary caregivers. As children, we naturally view our caregivers as the ultimate authority figures, and their beliefs or behaviors—whether healthy or distorted—shape our perceptions of ourselves and the world. When a caregiver instills distorted beliefs or devalues the child, these messages can become internalized as truth.

The authority bias is further compounded when the offender in an interpersonal trauma also wields power or influence, reinforcing harmful narratives such as unworthiness or shame. Survivors often struggle to disentangle their own sense of self from these externally imposed distortions, making it difficult to challenge or reject the harmful beliefs rooted in both early caregiving and abusive authority figures.

The challenge in therapy is not only to dismantle these beliefs but to do so with compassion, helping survivors shift the internalized authority from the abuser to themselves. Since trauma often occurs within the context of relationships, healing must also happen within relationships. A key part of this process is the compassionate challenge of distorted beliefs that have been shaped by authority figures, caregivers, or those who exerted power over the survivor in the past.

One common belief among survivors is that they are unworthy of love because of what they've endured. This belief is often reinforced by abusers or significant others who held power in the survivor's life, creating an authority bias —where survivors trust the offender's distorted messages about their value. The idea that they are fundamentally broken makes it hard to trust others, reinforcing the isolation and shame that keep them trapped. To begin healing, these beliefs need to be gently challenged through compassionate questioning.

The distortion from the offender in interpersonal trauma often leads survivors to believe that their value or worth is based solely on how they perform or what they can offer, rather than on their inherent self-worth. This skewed perception is deeply ingrained, as the offender may have manipulated the survivor into thinking that love or acceptance is conditional, tied to specific behaviors or acts. As a result, the survivor may develop a pattern of seeking approval or validation through performance, whether it be through achievements, people-pleasing, or fulfilling others' needs. This performative behavior becomes the "shiny object" that distracts them from their deeper emotional needs, making them believe that by excelling or conforming, they can earn love or worthiness. This leaves little room for authenticity and connection, perpetuating a cycle of disconnection from their true selves and from genuine, unconditional relationships.

In therapy, **Socratic questioning** serves as a powerful tool to guide survivors in examining the assumptions and beliefs that stem from their trauma. Socratic questioning is a structured yet flexible approach that allows survivors to explore their thoughts, feelings, and behaviors about their traumatic experiences without judgment. By asking open-ended questions, the therapist helps the survivor evaluate the authority of the beliefs that dominate their sense of self.

Here are the steps of Socratic questioning that help challenge these authority-driven beliefs:

1. IDENTIFY THE SOURCE OF THE BELIEF

The first step is to help the survivor understand where their belief originated. For example, if a survivor believes they are unworthy of love, the therapist might ask, "Where did you first learn that you are unlovable?" This question encourages the survivor to reflect on the source of the belief, often identifying that it stems from the abuser or a significant authority figure from their past. Recognizing that these beliefs come from an external authority rather than their own thoughts is the first step toward reclaiming their sense of self.

2. EVALUATE THE EVIDENCE

Once the source of the belief is identified, the next step is to question its validity. The therapist might ask, "What evidence do you have that supports this belief today?" This helps the survivor examine their current relationships and experiences. Often, survivors will realize that their present-day relationships contradict the old belief. By encouraging survivors to look for evidence that challenges the belief, the therapist helps them start to break free from the distorted authority of their past.

3. EXPLORE THE FUNCTION OF THE BELIEF

At this stage, the therapist guides the survivor in understanding why they hold on to the belief. "What purpose does this belief serve for you?" The survivor may recognize that the belief has served as a protective mechanism, guarding them from rejection or abandonment. This step helps the survivor differentiate between the belief's original function—protection in the face of trauma—and its current impact on their life, which may no longer be necessary or helpful.

4. CHALLENGE THE BELIEF WITH COMPASSION

Rather than confronting the belief head-on, the therapist invites the survivor to gently question its validity. A question like, "How true is this belief for you today?" allows the survivor to explore whether the belief still serves them or if it's holding them back. This compassionate approach avoids judgment and encourages the survivor to reflect on the belief from a place of curiosity. The therapist serves as a ¨fair witness¨, creating a non-judgmental space for exploration.

5. REWRITE THE NARRATIVE

As the belief is deconstructed, the survivor is encouraged to rewrite the narrative in a way that reflects their present reality. For instance, the belief "I am unworthy of love" can be transformed into "I am worthy of love, just as I am." The therapist helps the survivor integrate this new belief into their everyday life, reinforcing it through the evidence of their current relationships and experiences. This step allows the survivor to reclaim their authority over their narrative, no longer bound by the distorted voices of the past.

Challenging authority bias in trauma survivors requires sensitivity and patience. Survivors often hold tightly to the beliefs instilled by their abusers because they've been reinforced over time. However, by carefully guiding the survivor through Socratic questioning, the therapist helps them dismantle these beliefs and begin to trust their own voice. As survivors learn to question the authority of their abuser's voice, they start to recognize their own authority over their sense of self and worth.

Source bias also plays a significant role in shaping distorted beliefs. Survivors often accept the words of their abusers or significant authority figures as the ultimate truth, believing that the source of the message holds more weight than their own internal voice. This bias is particularly strong in those who have experienced grooming, where the abuser systematically undermines the survivor's sense of reality. As a result, survivors find it difficult to challenge these beliefs on their own, as they've been conditioned to trust the authority of the abuser over themselves.

The therapist's role is to help the survivor transition from relying on external sources of authority, such as the offender or past caregivers, to trusting their internal sense of self-worth. This shift begins with acknowledging the distorted messages ingrained by the offender, who often created a sense that the survivor's value was tied to performance. The first step is recognizing authority bias, where the survivor views the offender's words or actions as ultimate truth. The second step involves the therapist using Socratic questioning to gently challenge this bias by helping the survivor examine the source of their beliefs and consider alternative perspectives. Finally, the third step is guiding the survivor to internalize their own sense of authority—learning to trust their experiences, feelings, and self-perception. By gradually moving from external validation to an internal sense of self, survivors can reclaim their narrative and begin to break free from the need to perform as the "shiny object" to earn love or worth.

Through this process, survivors gradually dismantle the internalized authority of their past abusers and reclaim their sense of self. They learn that their worth is not determined by someone else's authority but by their inherent value as human beings. The therapist's gentle guidance in questioning these beliefs helps the survivor navigate the often-difficult terrain of self-discovery, leading to deeper healing and empowerment.

The process of challenging beliefs rooted in trauma also involves understanding how these beliefs function as self-protective mechanisms. Often, survivors cling to these beliefs because they serve as a buffer against further pain. For instance, the belief "I am unworthy of love" may protect the survivor from the fear of rejection. By holding on to this belief, the survivor avoids the risk of opening up to others, thereby avoiding potential hurt. However, as the therapist helps the survivor explore the origins and function of this belief, they come to understand that it is no longer necessary for their protection. In fact, it may be holding them back from forming meaningful relationships.

Once survivors recognize the protective function of their beliefs, they can begin to explore alternative ways of coping that don't involve self-deprecation or avoidance. This is where the "shiny object" comes into play. For many survivors, the shiny object represents the behaviors or achievements they've relied on to feel worthy or valued. Whether it's perfectionism, overachievement, or people-pleasing, these shiny objects serve as temporary fixes for deeper feelings of inadequacy. The therapist helps the survivor recognize that these behaviors are not the solution to their trauma—they are distractions from the underlying pain.

By shifting the focus from the shiny object to the root cause of the behavior, survivors begin to see that their worth is not tied to their performance or achievements. They learn to trust their authentic selves and let go of the need to prove their value through external validation. This shift allows survivors to embrace their vulnerability and open themselves up to healing relationships.

In conclusion, challenging authority bias and source bias in trauma survivors requires a compassionate, structured approach. Through the use of Socratic questioning, therapists can help survivors deconstruct the distorted beliefs instilled by their abusers and reclaim their sense of self-worth. By exploring the origins, function, and current relevance of these beliefs, survivors begin to trust their own voice and let go of the shiny objects that have kept them from healing. With curiosity and compassion as the guiding principles, survivors can rewrite their narratives and forge a path toward lasting recovery.

JOHN'S STORY; CHALLENGING THE NARRATIVE OF 'DAMAGED GOODS'

John's journey in therapy began with deep-seated feelings of shame, confusion, and conflict, rooted in his childhood trauma and perpetuated in his adult relationships. Over several sessions, we began to explore the connections between his painful past and his current behavior, particularly his reliance on sex workers, despite his love for his wife. The use of Socratic questioning became the key to unraveling the layers of belief and authority that had governed his life for so long, allowing John to confront the authority bias he had unknowingly adopted from his childhood experiences.

John had been sexually abused by his stepfather for several years. The abuse occurred several times a week, always under the cover of night, in the basement room where John slept—isolated from his brothers, who lived in other parts of the house. "What do you think it meant that your stepfather insisted on you having that room in the basement?" I asked one day, opening the door to what we both knew was a difficult subject.

"It made it easier for him," John said quietly. "I was out of sight. No one could hear me. It was like... I didn't exist to anyone else." His words revealed the first layer of authority bias—the way his stepfather had set the stage to dominate and control John's life, isolating him both physically and emotionally.

"And what about your mother?" I pressed gently. "How do you think her actions—or inactions—played into what was happening?"

John had always avoided this question. His mother was a complicated figure in his life, and while he had long since accepted that his stepfather was the source of his trauma, the silence of his mother had always been more difficult for him to confront. "I don't think she knew," he said, but his tone was hesitant.

"Is that what you think? Or is that what you want to believe?" I asked, guiding him to reflect on the truth of the situation.

John sat in silence for a long time before responding. "I don't know. How could she not know? I mean, I was always down there, and she never asked what was going on. She never came to check on me."

"So, what does that tell you?" I continued. "About how much your mother was paying attention to what was happening in your family?"

"It feels like she didn't care," he admitted. "Like she didn't want to see what was going on."

This was a turning point. For so long, John had held onto the belief that his mother's silence was ignorance, not indifference. But as we unpacked this belief, it became clear that her inaction had contributed to his feelings of abandonment and isolation. "So, if your mother wasn't protecting you, who was?" I asked.

"No one," John replied softly. "No one was."

"How do you think that shaped how you see yourself today?" I asked, nudging him toward the next layer of discovery.

John thought for a moment. "I guess I've always felt like I had to take care of myself. No one else would."

As we continued to explore this narrative, it became apparent that John had internalized the belief that his value was tied to how well he could perform, protect, and control situations—beliefs he had carried into his adult life. His use of sex workers, we discovered, was a way of asserting control over intimacy, mirroring the transactional nature of his relationship with his stepfather. "When you visit sex workers," I asked, "what do you feel you are controlling in that situation?"

"Everything," John said. "There's no emotional risk. I don't have to give anything of myself, and they can't hurt me."

"Does it remind you of anything?" I asked, guiding him to see the parallels between his past and present.

He was quiet for a long time. "It's like when I was a kid," he finally admitted. "With my stepfather, it was always about him taking what he wanted. But with the sex workers, I'm the one in control. It's like I'm rewriting what happened, but this time I'm the one with the power."

We explored this further, and John began to see how his behavior with sex workers wasn't just about physical satisfaction. It was about reenacting his trauma in a way that allowed him to feel in control—a defense mechanism that he had learned in childhood to protect himself from vulnerability.

As we delved deeper, I asked, "What does that mean for your relationship with your wife? If sex with the workers is about control, what does intimacy with your wife represent?"

John paused, clearly uncomfortable. "With her... it's different. It's real. I love her, but it's scary. I don't know if I can be enough for her. I'm always afraid she'll see what's wrong with me."

"And where does that fear come from?" I asked, challenging him to examine the source of his belief.

"It's like with my mom," John said, his voice breaking. "She didn't see me. She didn't protect me. If my own mother couldn't love me enough to keep me safe, how can my wife love me?"

We sat with that truth for a moment, allowing it to settle. "What if it's not about your mother or your stepfather anymore?" I asked. "What if your value isn't tied to what they did or didn't do?"

John looked up at me, uncertain. "What do you mean?"

"Your stepfather taught you to believe that your worth was transactional—that you had to give something or perform in a certain way to be valued," I explained. "And your mother's silence made you believe you weren't worth protecting. But what if they were wrong? What if your value isn't based on their actions or inactions?"

This was a pivotal moment in John's therapy. Slowly, he began to question the authority those figures had held over his life. "But I've always felt like what I do defines who I am," he said.

"Do you think that's true?" I asked. "Or is that a belief you inherited from them?"

Over time, through continued questioning and reflection, John began to see that the authority figures from his childhood—his stepfather and his mother—had distorted his sense of self. Their actions had shaped his belief that love was conditional and that his worth was based on performance. But now, in therapy, he was beginning to reclaim his narrative. "What if you trusted your own feelings and experiences?" I asked. "What if you became the authority in your own life, rather than letting their actions define you?"

Through this process, John started to see his behavior with sex workers for what it was—a way to avoid vulnerability, born from the distorted belief that real intimacy was dangerous and that his worth was based on what he could control. He also began to challenge his fear of being emotionally open with his wife, recognizing that his past didn't compromise his love for her but was something he could embrace without the need to perform or prove his value.

In the end, John's journey was one of reclaiming his sense of self, stepping out of the shadow of his stepfather's authority and his mother's inaction. By challenging the authority bias that had governed his beliefs for so long, he was finally able to see that his worth wasn't tied to his past—or to the performances that had defined so much of his adult life. He learned to trust his own experiences, to become the authority in his own story, and to build a future rooted in authenticity, vulnerability, and love.

Chapter 20

WHEN BOUNDARIES BLUR: THE IMPACT OF COUNTERTRANSFERENCE

In therapy, particularly when working with survivors of relational trauma, it is critical for therapists to recognize how their own beliefs, experiences, and biases can influence the therapeutic relationship. We all carry personal histories that shape our perspectives, and therapists are not exempt from this. These personal stories can subtly impact the dynamics of the therapist-client relationship. Acknowledging our distortions is vital because, without this awareness, we risk letting our own reactions become the "shiny object"—the focus of our attention—rather than the needs and experiences of the client. The ability to see beyond our own emotional responses allows us to remain true to the healing process, grounded in the client's needs.

Countertransference, which refers to the therapist's emotional reactions toward the client, can distort the therapeutic space if not managed appropriately. It emerges when therapists unconsciously project their own unresolved emotions or experiences onto the client. While transference is the client projecting feelings from past relationships onto the therapist, countertransference occurs when the therapist's reactions, influenced by their own personal history, affect the relationship. These dynamics, left unexamined, can become the "shiny object" that detracts from the therapeutic goals. Therefore, therapists must manage their countertransference carefully and be aware of how their emotional responses can skew the therapeutic process.

Haye´s model of managing countertransference involves cultivating five key qualities: self-insight, conceptualizing ability, empathy, self-integration, and anxiety management. Each of these is essential in navigating the therapeutic space with clarity and compassion. Understanding these qualities not only helps in managing countertransference but also enables therapists to be a fair witness to the client's journey, minimizing the potential for harm caused by personal biases.

1. SELF-INSIGHT: UNDERSTANDING ONE'S OWN BIASES

Self-insight is the foundation of managing countertransference. Therapists must develop a deep understanding of their thoughts, feelings, and biases to recognize when countertransference is occurring. This awareness requires ongoing self-reflection and the ability to notice when the client's narrative triggers personal emotional responses. Without this insight, the therapist may focus on the "shiny object" of their own emotional reactions—perhaps becoming overly sympathetic, judgmental, or distracted—rather than attending to the client's needs. Therapists must continually ask themselves whether their reactions are truly in service of the client's healing or a reflection of their unresolved issues.

2. CONCEPTUALIZING ABILITY: UNDERSTANDING THE RELATIONAL DYNAMICS

Once a therapist recognizes countertransference, they must also possess the ability to conceptualize what is happening within the therapeutic relationship. Conceptualizing ability allows therapists to step back and understand the relational dynamics at play, recognizing how past experiences are being projected and replayed in the therapy room. This is especially important when working with trauma survivors, as the therapist may unconsciously react to the client's behaviors through the lens of their own past. Without the ability to see the bigger picture, the therapist may become overly focused on the "shiny object" of the client's presenting behavior, losing sight of the deeper relational issues at play.

For example, if a trauma survivor presents with defensiveness or withdrawal, the therapist must understand these behaviors within the context of the client's history rather than react to them personally. By maintaining a clear conceptual understanding of the therapeutic dynamics, therapists can avoid becoming entangled in their own emotional responses and remain focused on the client's healing process.

3. EMPATHY: MAINTAINING EMOTIONAL ATTUNEMENT WITHOUT OVERWHELM

Empathy is a cornerstone of effective therapy and is crucial in managing countertransference. It allows therapists to attune to their clients' experiences and emotions without becoming overwhelmed by their own emotional responses. While empathy enables the therapist to connect with the client and validate their experiences, it also requires emotional boundaries to prevent the therapist from becoming overly immersed in the client's narrative.

In the context of countertransference, empathy must be carefully balanced. If a therapist becomes too emotionally involved, they may lose their ability to maintain a neutral and supportive stance, focusing instead on their emotional reactions—another example of the "shiny object" that distracts from the client's needs. Empathy, when managed well, helps the therapist remain present and connected without losing sight of the therapeutic goals.

4. SELF-INTEGRATION: EMBRACING VULNERABILITY AND AUTHENTICITY

Self-integration involves embracing the therapist's own experiences, emotions, and humanity within the therapeutic process. Therapists are human, and their emotional responses are inevitable. However, it is the ability to integrate these emotions into the therapeutic work in a way that benefits the client that is key. This integration requires therapists to acknowledge their vulnerabilities and remain authentic in the therapeutic relationship, while also maintaining the boundaries necessary to ensure that the therapy remains client-centered.

For instance, if a therapist is reminded of their own painful experiences by a client's story, acknowledging and processing these emotions outside the therapy room can prevent the therapist from allowing those emotions to dictate their responses in session. By being aware of their own vulnerabilities, therapists can create a space where they remain connected to the client's journey without allowing their own experiences to overshadow the client's narrative.

5. ANXIETY MANAGEMENT: STAYING PRESENT IN THE THERAPEUTIC SPACE

Finally, anxiety management is crucial for therapists to remain present and focused during sessions. When countertransference arises, it can provoke anxiety, as the therapist may feel discomfort, fear, or uncertainty about how to handle the situation. Managing this anxiety is essential for maintaining a calm and supportive presence in the therapy room.

If the therapist becomes overwhelmed by their anxiety, they may shift focus away from the client's needs, turning the client's experience into the "shiny object" that triggers the therapist's discomfort. Effective anxiety management allows therapists to sit with their own discomfort while continuing to focus on the client's healing. This requires developing healthy coping mechanisms, such as mindfulness or supervision, to ensure that the therapist's anxiety does not interfere with the therapeutic process.

Anxiety management for therapists becomes particularly crucial when a client becomes dysregulated during a session. In these moments, the client's intense emotional responses may trigger anxiety in the therapist, creating a sense of uncertainty about how to manage the situation. This internal anxiety can interfere with the therapist's ability to provide the containment and grounding that the client needs in that moment. If the therapist's anxiety goes unchecked, it may manifest as a desire to avoid difficult or emotionally charged topics in future sessions, fearing that the client will again become dysregulated.

This avoidance, though stemming from a place of concern, can undermine the therapeutic process, preventing the client from fully exploring and processing important but painful material. To manage these situations, the therapist must practice self-regulation techniques, such as grounding, mindfulness, and deep breathing, to remain calm and present. By managing their own anxiety, the therapist can create a safe space for the client, allowing them to explore difficult emotions without fear of being overwhelmed or abandoned in the process. This presence builds trust and enables deeper healing as the client feels supported even in their most dysregulated states.

ADDRESSING COUNTERTRANSFERENCE THROUGH REFLECTION AND SUPERVISION

Recognizing and managing countertransference is not a solitary task. It often requires external reflection, particularly through supervision. In supervision, therapists can explore their emotional reactions, gain insight into the dynamics of their therapeutic relationships, and receive feedback on how to manage countertransference. Group supervision, in particular, offers the benefit of multiple perspectives, allowing therapists to see their blind spots and gain a clearer understanding of their reactions.

Through supervision, therapists can explore whether their emotional responses are disproportionate to the client's behavior and gain new insights into their own relational patterns. This reflective process helps therapists recognize when the "shiny object" of their own emotional reactions is detracting from the client's healing journey. By engaging in regular supervision, therapists can ensure that they are providing the best possible care for their clients while also attending to their own emotional needs.

FOSTERING A COLLABORATIVE HEALING PROCESS

Ultimately, managing countertransference is about fostering a therapeutic environment that is both compassionate and self-aware. By recognizing their own biases and emotional reactions, therapists can create a space where clients feel safe to explore their trauma without fear of being judged or misunderstood. When therapists approach the therapeutic relationship with humility, curiosity, and self-reflection, they are better equipped to support clients on their journey toward healing.

The therapeutic relationship is a dynamic and evolving process that requires constant attention and care. By cultivating the qualities of self-insight, conceptualizing ability, empathy, self-integration, and anxiety management, therapists can navigate the complexities of countertransference with integrity. This allows them to remain focused on the client's needs, avoiding the distraction of the "shiny object" of their own emotional responses, and ultimately supporting the client's growth and empowerment in their healing journey.

CONTAINING THE CHAOS: COUNTERTRANSFERENCE AND SELF-REFLECTION IN THERAPEUTIC PRACTICE

John had been coming to therapy for a while, and we had explored many facets of his trauma, including the years of abuse by his stepfather and his struggle with using sex workers, which he felt conflicted with his love for his wife. It had been a long and emotionally charged journey, filled with moments of insight, shame, and slow healing. But today was different. Today, his wife had joined the session for the first time, and the purpose was to open a door for empathy and understanding between them. Yet, as soon as she began speaking, it became clear this would not be easy.

Sitting across from John, his wife's words started to shift from expression to accusation. "I just don't understand," she began, voice quivering with hurt and confusion. "What kind of man does this? Is it because of what happened to you? Are you... gay? Or are you just a pervert? Sleeping with sex workers, lying to me... who does that?"

As her words intensified, I felt a deep sense of discomfort rising within me. John sat in silence, his eyes downcast, seemingly shrinking into himself with every harsh word. The energy in the room was palpable, a mix of pain, anger, and unspoken fear. My instinct as a therapist was to protect John, to step in and shield him from the verbal blows that I knew were reinforcing his long-held belief that he was defective, unworthy, and fundamentally broken. His wife's accusations were precisely what we had been working through in private sessions—John's internalized sense of defectiveness, the very thing that had kept him trapped in silence and shame for years.

But there was also his wife, clearly in pain, lashing out from a place of betrayal, confusion, and hurt. She needed space to express her feelings, to have her own story heard. Yet, my countertransference was becoming strong—my own emotional reactions to the situation were surfacing, rooted in a desire to do it "right" and not let this moment spiral into further harm for John. This was where managing my own anxiety became crucial, recognizing that my need to protect John could easily silence his wife, which could perpetuate the distance between them, and potentially between myself and her as well.

The first step was **self-insight**—acknowledging that my countertransference fueled my desire to protect John. His wife's words were harsh, but they mirrored the same internal dialogue that had plagued John for years. I realized I wasn't just feeling protective of John; I was also grappling with my anxiety about how to manage the session without letting it cause harm. My own fear of failing as a therapist was at play, and I needed to separate that from what was unfolding in the room.

Next came **conceptualizing ability**—understanding the dynamics between John and his wife, and between both of them and myself. I needed to frame what was happening in the larger context of their relationship. His wife was expressing fear and pain, trying to understand how John's past trauma intersected with his behavior, while John was retreating, unable to respond. I recognized that I was becoming part of the relational triangle, feeling pulled to side with John as the victim, but that would only perpetuate the sense that his wife was the enemy. My task was to remain balanced, facilitating the conversation without allowing my emotions to interfere.

The third element was **empathy,** for both John and his wife. I had to connect to her pain while also understanding the deep wounds John carried. Empathy didn't mean condoning her words, but it did mean creating space for her emotions to surface without shutting them down. It meant showing her that I understood her hurt, while also recognizing the risk this posed to John. It required delicate navigation—acknowledging her feelings without allowing them to become weapons that might retraumatize John. This empathy was a balancing act, a careful dance between both parties.

Then came **self-integration**—bringing my own experiences and emotional reactions into the process without letting them overwhelm the situation. I had to hold my desire to intervene in check. I could feel my anxiety growing as John remained silent, but I needed to trust the process. My role wasn't to fix the situation in that moment, but to provide a space where both John and his wife could confront their own pain. I needed to show that I could tolerate the discomfort in the room, which would model for John and his wife that they, too, could tolerate the hard truths they were confronting.

Finally, **anxiety management** came into play. The tension in the room was thick, and I was acutely aware of how easily this could go wrong. The fear that John would withdraw, that his wife would walk away feeling unheard, and that I would somehow fail them both was intense. But managing my own anxiety meant staying grounded, taking deep breaths, and trusting my training. I had to let go of the need for an immediate solution and instead focus on containing the emotions in the room, giving both John and his wife the opportunity to be heard without letting the session unravel.

As the session continued, I gently intervened, asking his wife to pause for a moment and inviting John to share what he was feeling. I used **Socratic questioning,** carefully exploring with John what it meant to him to hear his wife's fears, and what was behind her accusations. "John, when you hear your wife say these things, what comes up for you? What do you think she's really afraid of?" His answer revealed layers of fear—not just of judgment, but of losing his wife's love altogether. The shiny object of his behavior—the use of sex workers—was about more than sex; it was about trying to control something in his life when everything else felt out of control.

At the same time, I asked his wife, "When you call him those names, what do you hope will happen? What do you fear if you don't express this anger in this way?" Her answer was about fear—fear of being betrayed again, fear of not understanding the man she married.

By containing both of their emotions and guiding them through the process, we were able to navigate the session without it escalating into further harm. My countertransference, though present, had been managed through self-awareness and a commitment to empathy and curiosity. Both John and his wife left the session having expressed their pain, but also having heard each other, perhaps for the first time in a long time.

This session was a reminder of the complexity of working with relational trauma, and how the therapist's own reactions can either hinder or help the process. Managing countertransference requires constant reflection and the ability to hold space for all emotions—without becoming overwhelmed by them.

Chapter 21

UNCOVERING THE INVISIBLE THREADS: FORMULATING A HYPOTHESES TO LINK PAST TRAUMA TO PRESENT BEHAVIOR

In therapeutic practice, developing a hypothesis that connects past trauma to present compulsive behaviors is essential for effective treatment. Clients often struggle to understand how past events influence their current behaviors, especially when there isn't an obvious, direct link to their trauma narrative. Using the term "hypothesis" with clients is particularly helpful, as it implies that evidence is needed to support it, and it encourages an open, curious mindset. This approach shifts the focus from judgment, which often leads to shame, toward curiosity and understanding, empowering clients to explore the underlying motivations behind their behaviors. A hypothesis invites collaboration and allows room for adjustment, helping both the therapist and the client stay open to new insights and changes in the healing process.

The premise that all behavior has meaning is central to therapeutic exploration. By approaching compulsive behaviors through the lens of safety and coping mechanisms, therapists can guide clients toward understanding their actions with compassion. In doing so, clients are more likely to engage with their behaviors thoughtfully, rather than viewing them as failures or moral shortcomings. This approach is especially effective when paired with models like the Stages of Change, which helps assess a client's readiness to address their trauma and associated behaviors.

STAGES OF CHANGE AND HYPOTHESIS DEVELOPMENT

The Stages of Change model provides a structured way to gauge where a client is in their process of change, helping the therapist craft hypotheses that fit their current mindset. The five stages—precontemplation, contemplation, preparation, action, and maintenance—are useful for guiding therapeutic interventions.

1. Precontemplation: In this stage, clients may not yet acknowledge that their trauma has impacted their behavior. A hypothesis here might center on raising awareness without pushing for change. For instance, a client might deny the connection between their past abuse and their difficulty maintaining intimate relationships. The therapist can introduce gentle curiosity, asking, "Could there be a link between your past experiences and how you feel now?" This helps the client begin to consider the possibility without feeling forced to take immediate action.

2. Contemplation: Clients in this stage recognize the problem but are ambivalent about change. The therapist can offer a hypothesis to deepen their exploration. For example, "Could the secrecy surrounding your trauma be influencing your current need to hide aspects of your life?" This invites clients to reflect on their behaviors in light of their trauma, fostering curiosity about the potential connections.

3. Preparation: Once clients are preparing for change, the therapist can propose more specific hypotheses. At this stage, a hypothesis may explore how certain behaviors serve a coping function. For example, a client who uses compulsive behaviors like pornography might benefit from exploring the hypothesis, "Does using pornography help manage feelings of anxiety or emotional overwhelm related to your trauma?"

4. Action: In this stage, clients actively work toward change. Hypotheses at this point should be clear and testable, helping clients track their progress. For example, "Does your urge to engage in compulsive behavior increase when you're feeling emotionally disconnected from your partner?" This helps clients identify patterns in their behavior, empowering them to intervene before acting on their compulsions.

5. Maintenance: In the maintenance stage, clients work to sustain the changes they've made. The therapist can help by creating hypotheses that reinforce these positive changes. For instance, "When you practice open communication, does it reduce your urge to act out compulsively?" This supports clients in identifying what's working and strengthens their ongoing recovery.

HYPOTHESIS IN PRACTICE: EXPLORING THE ROOTS OF BEHAVIOR

A practical example of hypothesis testing in therapy comes from a client struggling with compulsive lying, particularly within his long-term relationship. The client, Carlos, had been lying to his wife for years, often about insignificant matters that didn't seem to benefit him. When we explored this behavior, Carlos shared that his mother encouraged a relationship with a mentor after his parents' divorce. This mentor later initiated a sexual relationship with him, which Carlos had kept secret.

Initially, Carlos did not recognize the relationship as abuse, but through therapy, he began to see the harmful dynamics at play, particularly the secrecy surrounding the relationship. The therapist hypothesized that the secrecy of his childhood experience was influencing his current need to lie. By connecting the dots between secrecy in his youth and secrecy in his adult relationships, Carlos began to understand that his compulsive lying was a learned behavior rooted in his trauma. Testing this hypothesis allowed Carlos to see patterns of secrecy throughout his life, moving him from the contemplation to the action stage of change.

ADDRESSING DISPROPORTIONATE REACTIONS

When creating a hypothesis, it's important to assess whether a client's reactions are disproportionate to the current situation. Disproportionate emotional responses often signal that past trauma is being triggered. A useful tool for this is the "affect bridge," where clients identify current feelings and connect them to past experiences that evoke similar emotions. For instance, if Carlos felt extreme anxiety when his wife asked simple questions, we might explore whether this anxiety mirrors the fear and secrecy he felt as a child in the abusive relationship. This process highlights how past trauma can disproportionately influence current behavior.

HYPOTHESES AND ATTEMPTS TO CHANGE

Another critical aspect of formulating hypotheses is recognizing when clients have tried to change a behavior but have been unsuccessful. When a behavior persists despite efforts to stop it, it often serves a deeper, unrecognized function. Exploring the potential benefits of the behavior—such as anxiety relief—can help clients approach it with curiosity rather than shame.

For example, Carlos's use of pornography was a source of deep shame. However, when we framed the behavior as potentially helpful in some way, he began to explore its function. Through Socratic questioning, Carlos realized that his pornography use was a way to cope with feelings of inadequacy and emotional overwhelm. By helping him see the behavior as a tool for managing difficult emotions, the hypothesis allowed him to approach the behavior without self-condemnation, opening the door to change.

RECOGNIZING DISSOCIATION IN COMPULSIVE BEHAVIOR

In some cases, clients may engage in behaviors while feeling dissociated, disconnected from their actions. This cognitive dissociation can manifest as a loss of control, where clients describe their actions as automatic or robotic. Such dissociative behaviors often indicate that the client is avoiding confronting painful emotions or memories related to trauma.

In Carlos's case, he sometimes described feeling detached from his actions, especially when engaging in compulsive behaviors like lying or pornography use. The therapist hypothesized that this dissociation served to protect Carlos from confronting unresolved feelings of shame and fear related to his trauma. By recognizing this dissociation, we were able to incorporate it into the larger hypothesis, helping Carlos understand that these behaviors weren't merely compulsive—they were strategies for avoiding emotional pain.

TESTING THE HYPOTHESIS

Once a hypothesis has been formed, it's essential to test it in real-time. For Carlos, this involved becoming aware of moments when he felt the urge to lie or engage in pornography and checking in with his emotional state at the time. Was he feeling anxious, disconnected, or overwhelmed? Was there a pattern linking these feelings to his trauma? As Carlos tracked these moments, he began to see how his compulsive behaviors were attempts to manage his emotional state rather than being random or morally flawed actions.

Testing the hypothesis helped Carlos shift his focus from feeling ashamed of his behavior to understanding its function in his life. This deeper understanding empowered him to address the root causes of his behavior, fostering lasting change.

CONCLUSION: HYPOTHESIS BUILDING AS A PATH TO HEALING

Developing a hypothesis to link past trauma to present compulsive behavior is a dynamic process that evolves as clients move through the stages of change. By framing behaviors as meaningful rather than shameful, therapists can guide clients toward curiosity and self-compassion. Whether through assessing disproportionate reactions, exploring dissociation, or examining attempts to change, the hypothesis serves as a powerful tool for understanding and ultimately transforming behaviors rooted in trauma.

This approach allows clients to take ownership of their healing, moving from a place of avoidance and shame to one of insight and action. By testing hypotheses in real-life situations, clients can see the connections between their past and present, empowering them to make meaningful changes and move forward in their recovery.

Chapter 22

FROM CONFLICT TO CONNECTION: NAVIGATING THE PATH TO REPAIR

The ability to repair disruptions in relationships is essential, particularly in therapeutic work with trauma survivors. All relationships—whether personal or professional—inevitably encounter moments of conflict or misunderstanding. Recognizing these disruptions and addressing them thoughtfully is crucial for building trust and fostering healing. For a therapist acting as a fair witness, it's not about avoiding disruption but about how effectively the repair is made afterward. The goal is to strengthen the relationship through understanding and reconciliation.

For trauma survivors, these disruptions often hit harder because of their history of betrayal, abandonment, or abuse. Small relational fractures can trigger feelings of deep insecurity and fear. A fair witness must first acknowledge the survivor's feelings and recognize the specific impact that the disruption has had on them. By doing so, the therapist communicates empathy and an understanding of the survivor's heightened sensitivities, helping the survivor feel seen and validated. This empathetic approach shifts the dynamic from focusing on the problem to focusing on the solution, making repair the central goal.

NAVIGATING DISRUPTION WITHOUT DEFENSIVENESS

The shiny object here might be the therapist's own instinct to "do it right," or to protect the client from further harm. When a rupture occurs, it is easy for the therapist to feel defensive or anxious about how to manage the situation. This reaction, though well-intentioned, can hinder the therapist's ability to remain present and supportive. Instead of falling into defensiveness, the therapist must view the disruption as an opportunity for growth and deeper connection. The goal is not to avoid mistakes but to model the process of repair. By embracing the discomfort that comes with these moments, both the therapist and the client can deepen their understanding of each other and strengthen their bond.

Disruptions are not just about the client's reactions—they often reflect the therapist's own emotions and struggles. For example, in couples therapy with John, his wife began to express anger and frustration, calling him names and accusing him of being a pervert for using sex workers. As the therapist, I felt the urge to protect John from the accusations, knowing how they might reinforce his feelings of shame and defectiveness. However, stepping in too quickly or taking sides could invalidate the wife's experience and prevent her from expressing her emotions. Here, the therapist's own internal shiny object may be the desire to "fix" the situation immediately, rather than allowing the conversation to unfold naturally.

THE POWER OF VULNERABILITY IN REPAIR

Handling these ruptures involves creating space for both parties to express themselves while keeping the overall goal of repair in mind. It's important for the therapist to allow difficult emotions to surface, while remaining steady and containing the intensity of the moment. The therapist's role is to help the couple understand that expressing anger or frustration is a part of healing, as long as it leads to productive conversation and growth.

The moment of repair is not just about managing the disruption; it is also about teaching the survivor how to repair relationships outside of therapy. Survivors of trauma, especially those who have experienced betrayal, often struggle to trust others. By showing that relationships can withstand conflict and be repaired, the therapist is modeling resilience and trustworthiness. This teaches the survivor that not all disruptions are permanent, and that it is possible to rebuild connection even after a rupture.

ACKNOWLEDGING THE THERAPIST'S OWN EXPERIENCE

Disruptions don't only affect the client—they affect the therapist as well. It's essential for the therapist to recognize their own emotions during these moments. The therapist may feel frustration, helplessness, or even fear of making things worse. In John's case, his wife's accusations triggered a sense of urgency in me, as the therapist, to protect him. It's natural to feel the impulse to protect a vulnerable client, but it's also important to recognize when this impulse stems from the therapist's own fears of inadequacy or failure. By being mindful of these reactions, the therapist can stay grounded and avoid reacting impulsively.

Therapists must engage in self-reflection to understand how their own biases and emotions impact the therapeutic process. This self-awareness allows the therapist to manage their countertransference—

ensuring that their personal feelings do not interfere with the client's healing process. In John's case, managing my own anxiety was key to helping both him and his wife navigate their painful emotions and find a way forward. By acknowledging my own internal shiny object—the desire to "fix" things—I could refocus on facilitating meaningful dialogue, rather than rushing toward a premature resolution.

REPAIR AS A PATH TO GROWTH

When handled effectively, disruptions can actually serve as catalysts for growth. By addressing ruptures head-on, the therapist teaches the survivor that conflict doesn't have to mean the end of a relationship. In fact, it can open the door to greater intimacy and understanding. For trauma survivors, who may have experienced chronic betrayal or abandonment, learning how to repair relationships is a powerful tool for healing.

In moments of rupture, the therapist helps the client reflect on their own needs and feelings, while also encouraging them to listen to others. This collaborative process strengthens the therapeutic relationship and models healthy communication patterns. By guiding the client through these difficult moments, the therapist helps them learn that they can voice their needs, express their emotions, and still maintain connection with others.

EMPOWERMENT THROUGH REPAIR

Ultimately, the process of repair is about empowerment. When a survivor learns that they can express their hurt and still be heard, valued, and respected, it transforms their view of relationships. They begin to see themselves as worthy of care and attention, even when things go wrong. This is especially important for trauma survivors, who often carry a deep sense of unworthiness or fear of rejection.

The therapist's role in the repair process is to empower the survivor to take an active role in mending the relationship. This shifts the focus from the disruption itself to the survivor's ability to navigate and overcome it. In John's case, his ability to express his own vulnerability and understand his wife's perspective was crucial to rebuilding trust. By guiding him through this process, he was able to see that repair is possible, even in the face of significant challenges.

In conclusion, the ability to repair disruptions is central to being a fair witness in therapy. It requires patience, empathy, and a willingness to engage with the discomfort that comes with conflict. By focusing on repair rather than blame, the therapist can help the survivor feel empowered and capable of maintaining meaningful relationships, both in and out of therapy. This shift from seeing disruptions as failures to viewing them as opportunities for growth is a key component of the healing process.

Chapter 23

CREATING A SAFE THERAPEUTIC SPACE: WHY PREDICTABILITY MATTERS IN TRAUMA RECOVERY

In the journey of healing from relational sexual trauma, establishing trust and vulnerability is critical. Survivors often come from environments where unpredictability and unreliability were the norms, particularly in relationships with offenders and others around them. These experiences leave deep scars, making it difficult for survivors to trust others or engage in vulnerable interactions. As a result, building a reliable and predictable therapeutic relationship becomes one of the most essential elements in fostering safety and healing.

Many survivors have encountered situations where promises were made but not kept, leading to feelings of betrayal and mistrust. A common example of this might be when someone says, "I won't be mad if you don't want to talk about this," and then later uses the avoidance against the survivor, manipulating them emotionally. Another situation might involve a promise of confidentiality that is later broken, leaving the survivor feeling exposed and betrayed. Such experiences reinforce the survivor's belief that people cannot be trusted, further isolating them from seeking support.

For a therapist, becoming a steady and reliable presence is crucial in helping survivors rebuild their ability to trust. The therapeutic space must be consistent, transparent, and empowering, allowing the survivor to feel safe enough to explore their emotions without fear of judgment or manipulation. This consistent reliability reduces the survivor's anxiety, making it easier for them to open up and engage in the healing process.

BUILDING TRUST AFTER BROKEN PROMISES

Survivors of relational sexual trauma are often familiar with broken promises, and these breaches of trust can create lasting damage. For example, a survivor might confide in someone about their need for safety and request that certain aspects of their trauma remain unspoken, only to later find that this boundary was crossed and used against them. These moments reinforce the survivor's feelings of vulnerability and mistrust, making it harder for them to engage in future relationships, including the therapeutic one.

In contrast, when therapists and other supporters keep their word, respect boundaries, and demonstrate consistent support, the survivor can begin to rebuild their trust in others. This reliability becomes a foundation for survivors to feel secure enough to gradually lower their defenses and engage in the vulnerable work of trauma recovery. Therapists who model this reliability demonstrate to survivors that they are valued, respected, and supported, which is crucial in undoing the damage caused by past unreliable relationships.

NAVIGATING AVOIDANCE AND AUTONOMY IN THERAPY

A common challenge in working with trauma survivors is balancing the need to confront avoidance with respecting the survivor's autonomy. Survivors may avoid discussing certain aspects of their trauma because it feels too painful or overwhelming. However, pushing them too hard to confront these issues can backfire, leading to further avoidance or even a rupture in the therapeutic relationship.

One way to navigate this challenge is by consistently applying a lens of curiosity. For instance, a therapist might introduce the idea that the survivor's current struggles may be linked to past trauma, inviting the survivor to explore the connection without pressure. This approach allows the survivor to engage with their trauma at their own pace, fostering a sense of safety and predictability in the therapeutic relationship.

By maintaining a consistent approach grounded in empathy and curiosity, therapists create an environment where survivors feel supported in exploring difficult topics without feeling forced or rushed. This predictable approach helps survivors trust that their therapist will respect their boundaries while encouraging them to move forward in their healing journey.

BALANCING FLEXIBILITY AND CONSISTENCY IN THERAPY

Reliability and predictability do not mean rigidity. In fact, flexibility is an important aspect of therapeutic relationships, especially when it comes to accommodating the survivor's needs and preferences. However, flexibility must be balanced with consistency to maintain the survivor's sense of safety and trust.

For example, if a therapist needs to make changes to the schedule, it's important to communicate these changes openly and provide alternative options, while also acknowledging how the survivor might feel about the disruption. By giving the survivor a voice in how to navigate the change, the therapist demonstrates respect for the survivor's autonomy and helps to maintain the integrity of the therapeutic relationship.

Maintaining reliability in the therapeutic setting means that the survivor knows what to expect and can rely on the therapist to be transparent and accountable. This consistency helps reduce the anxiety that many survivors feel when engaging in vulnerable work. It also models healthy relational dynamics, showing the survivor that relationships can be both flexible and dependable.

CREATING A SAFE SPACE FOR HEALING

Survivors of relational sexual trauma need more than just words to feel safe—they need consistent actions that demonstrate care, empathy, and reliability. Trust is not given automatically, especially in the therapeutic context. It's important to acknowledge at the onset that there is no expectation for the client to trust the therapist simply because they are a therapist. Trust must be earned through actions, not words. This means the therapist must consistently honor the survivor's boundaries, respect their needs, and support them without judgment or manipulation. Over time, through reliable and predictable behavior, the survivor can begin to feel they can depend on the therapist, slowly building the foundation of safety and trust that is essential for healing.

By creating a space where survivors feel valued and supported, therapists help them rebuild their ability to trust others and engage in meaningful relationships. The reliability and predictability of the therapeutic relationship become the bedrock upon which survivors can process their trauma, explore their emotions, and begin to heal.

In summary, the reliable and predictable nature of relationships is vital for survivors of relational sexual trauma. Therapists play a crucial role in modeling these qualities, providing a safe and supportive environment where survivors can begin to rebuild trust in themselves and others. Through clear communication, consistent actions, and a focus on empathy and respect, therapists help survivors heal from the damage of past relationships and reclaim their sense of agency.

Chapter 24

CREATING A SHARED REALITY: BRIDGING PAST TRAUMA AND PRESENT PERCEPTION

Mirroring, in the context of therapy, plays a vital role in helping clients recognize attunement between their emotions, thoughts, and reactions to past trauma. When therapists mirror both the emotional and cognitive aspects of a client's experience, they validate the client's feelings and demonstrate an understanding of why they may feel the way they do, particularly based on old data or past experiences. For many trauma survivors, the emotions they experience in the present are often disproportionate to current events, as they are rooted in past trauma. The process of mirroring helps clients realize this link and opens up the possibility of challenging outdated responses that no longer serve them.

By validating the survivor's emotional experience—"It makes sense you feel this way given what you've been through"—therapists can reflect that the emotional response is expected based on the client's past. This acknowledgment is crucial because it helps the client feel understood and not judged for their reactions, which are often shaped by trauma. However, once this attunement and validation take place, it becomes possible to gently introduce the idea of challenging the old data by reflecting on the current situation. For instance, after validating an emotional response, the therapist can explore whether the intensity of the reaction fits the present-day event: "Given the data from your past, it's understandable that you'd feel this way, but let's take a look at what's happening right now. Do the facts of today support this level of emotional reaction?"

This process invites the client to begin discerning between what is a trauma-driven response and what is appropriate for the current situation. By using mirroring as a way to align both emotional attunement and cognitive reflection, the therapist helps the client pause and reconsider whether their response is proportionate to the reality of today. It's not about denying the client's feelings or dismissing their experience but providing them with the opportunity to assess whether their reactions are still useful or necessary. This helps them to challenge the automatic, trauma-related patterns that may no longer be helpful in their present lives.

Having a shared reality with the client is also essential in this process. As the therapist mirrors the client's experience, they can incorporate clarifying statements like, "Just to make sure I understand you correctly, you mean..." or "Point of clarification, you're saying that you feel... because...?" These statements are not only ways for the therapist to confirm their understanding but also provide the client with the opportunity to correct or clarify their thoughts and emotions. This creates a dialogue in which the client feels fully heard and understood, while also offering space to adjust or reframe their narrative in real-time.

This back-and-forth exchange fosters cognitive attunement. The therapist reflects the emotional truth of the client's experience while simultaneously inviting the client to engage in cognitive reflection: "Is what I'm feeling in this moment truly based on what's happening now, or is it rooted in past trauma?" This process helps the client to explore and adjust their perceptions and emotional responses, allowing for greater emotional regulation.

In a therapeutic relationship, attunement has two crucial components: affective attunement (emotional connection) and cognitive attunement (shared understanding and reflection). The combination of both allows the therapist and client to work together toward creating congruency between the client's internal world and external experiences. When the client's thinking is in line with their emotional reactions, and those reactions are appropriate to the current environment or situation, they begin to respond to the world in a more balanced and measured way.

This congruence, or alignment, is a key marker of healing from trauma, especially when addressing post-traumatic stress disorder (PTSD). For many trauma survivors, the intensity of their emotional responses is disproportionate to the current triggers because their minds and bodies are still reacting to past trauma. Through affective and cognitive attunement, the therapist helps the client shift from overreacting to neutral events to responding in a way that matches the reality of the present.

For example, if a client feels intense fear or panic in a relatively safe situation, the therapist's role is to first validate that fear (emotional attunement) but then encourage the client to reflect on whether the current threat is as real as it feels (cognitive attunement). Through this exploration, the client learns to regulate their responses, aligning their emotional reaction with the actual level of threat or challenge in the current environment. This process is fundamental to moving out of trauma-driven patterns and into a more grounded, present-focused way of living, reducing the intensity and frequency of PTSD symptoms.

In summary, mirroring through both emotional and cognitive attunement enables clients to recognize the validity of their feelings based on old trauma while offering them the opportunity to challenge those feelings based on the realities of today. The therapist's ability to reflect, clarify, and create a shared understanding with the client empowers them to align their thoughts, emotions, and reactions in a way that is proportionate to current situations. This congruency is essential for reducing trauma-related symptoms and helping the client live more fully in the present, rather than reacting to the past.

Chapter 25

THE POWER OF OPTIMISM AND POST-TRAUMATIC GROWTH IN HEALING TRAUMA

The ability to remain optimistic is a crucial element in supporting trauma survivors, particularly those who feel defective or broken due to their experiences. Many survivors believe there is no hope for recovery, viewing themselves as irreparably damaged. In these moments, it is essential for the therapist, as a fair witness, to embody optimism and recognize the survivor's inherent resilience. This hopeful outlook becomes a foundation upon which the survivor can begin to believe in their potential for healing and growth.

Optimism in therapy is not just about providing comfort or reassurance; it's about creating an environment where the survivor feels empowered to see that recovery is possible. The fair witness holds space for both the pain and the potential, acknowledging the survivor's very real challenges while emphasizing their capacity for transformation. Even in the face of the deepest trauma, there exists a spark of resilience. The therapist's role is to nurture this spark into a flame of hope and guide the survivor toward healing.

Optimism plays a critical role in countering the feelings of despair that often accompany trauma. It provides survivors with a lifeline, a reminder that healing is achievable even when it feels distant or impossible. The fair witness helps survivors understand that the journey toward recovery is rarely linear. There will be setbacks, but each challenge is also an opportunity for growth, learning, and strengthening of resilience.

A key aspect of healing from trauma is recognizing and embracing post-traumatic growth, the idea that through adversity, individuals can experience profound personal development. Post-traumatic growth occurs when survivors begin to find meaning and new perspectives after trauma, often leading to greater emotional strength, deepened relationships, and a renewed sense of purpose. This growth is not automatic; it is cultivated through the therapeutic process, particularly when optimism and hope are consistently reinforced.

Through optimism, challenges are reframed not as signs of failure, but as opportunities for resilience and personal evolution. This outlook encourages survivors to approach their struggles with curiosity and openness, rather than fear or self-judgment. With the guidance of the therapist, survivors can begin to see that adversity, rather than being something to avoid or fear, can be a catalyst for transformation and growth.

Central to this process is helping survivors connect their past experiences with their present behaviors. Often, survivors respond to current situations using outdated coping mechanisms from their trauma, reacting as though they are still in danger. The fair witness helps them understand these patterns, making it clear that these responses, while no longer helpful, once served a critical purpose in their survival. This realization fosters self-compassion and allows survivors to view themselves not as damaged, but as individuals who adapted to trauma and now have the capacity to heal and grow.

In addition to fostering understanding, the therapist plays a key role in supporting the survivor's post-traumatic growth. As survivors begin to recognize the impact of their trauma on their present behavior, they also start to see the possibility for growth beyond the trauma. The therapist encourages them to look for ways in which their experiences may have fostered strengths—whether in emotional resilience, empathy for others, or an ability to navigate adversity. By focusing on these emerging strengths, the survivor starts to develop a new, empowered narrative.

The therapist's unwavering belief in the survivor's potential for post-traumatic growth becomes a powerful tool in the healing process. The survivor, in turn, begins to internalize this belief and cultivate their own sense of hope. Recovery no longer seems like an unreachable goal; instead, it becomes a dynamic process in which the survivor can actively engage, even finding new purpose and meaning in life as they move beyond the pain of the past.

Connecting the past to the present is also essential for helping survivors realize that their trauma responses, though maladaptive now, were once protective. By reframing these behaviors as adaptive responses to past trauma, the therapist helps the survivor develop a more compassionate view of themselves. This reframing allows survivors to acknowledge their inherent resilience, recognize their ability to change, and cultivate a sense of hope and optimism for the future.

The therapist's role in this process is to provide consistent validation and support, reinforcing the survivor's capacity for both healing and growth. Through this collaboration, the survivor begins to see that their journey is not just about overcoming trauma but about emerging stronger and more self-aware as a result of it. This process embodies the essence of post-traumatic growth, where survivors not only heal but also transform their understanding of themselves and the world around them.

Belief in the potential success and growth of the survivor is at the heart of the fair witness's approach. This belief is not merely an abstract idea but is reflected in every therapeutic interaction, every moment of empathy, and every instance of encouragement. As the fair witness radiates optimism and hope, the survivor begins to internalize these qualities, gradually building belief in themselves and their ability to grow through adversity.

By maintaining an optimistic outlook and recognizing the potential for post-traumatic growth, therapists help survivors rewrite their trauma narratives. Instead of being defined by their past, survivors begin to see themselves as resilient, capable individuals who have the power to heal and thrive. The fair witness's unwavering faith in the survivor's potential for growth becomes a mirror, reflecting back the survivor's own worth, strength, and ability to embrace a future filled with possibility and renewal.

In the end, optimism, along with all the other essential characteristics of being a fair witness, becomes a powerful force in the therapist's work with trauma survivors. As a fair witness, the therapist not only offers unwavering belief in the survivor's capacity to heal but also embodies qualities like empathy, reliability, curiosity, and the ability to challenge harmful beliefs with compassion. This holistic approach fosters an environment where trust, safety, and connection can flourish, allowing post-traumatic growth to take root.

FRAMEWORK AND GUARDRAILS: NAVIGATING THE HEALING JOURNEY

Throughout *Beyond the Shiny Object*, we have explored how understanding trauma and its manifestations requires a deeper dive beneath the surface behaviors that often distract both survivors and those supporting them. This book has provided a set of frameworks or "guardrails" to guide therapists, partners, loved ones, and survivors in navigating the complexity of trauma healing.

These guardrails ensure that the focus remains on addressing the root causes of trauma, not just its symptoms. We've explored how to formulate hypotheses that connect past trauma to present behaviors, how to challenge beliefs with compassion, and how to recognize when coping mechanisms, such as the "shiny object," serve a deeper function. These frameworks are intended to provide clarity, structure, and direction for both the therapist and the survivor, ensuring that the healing journey is grounded in understanding and empathy rather than judgment.

At the core of this therapeutic process lies the role of the "fair witness". The fair witness is not just an observer but an active, compassionate participant in the survivor's healing journey. Each characteristic of the fair witness—authenticity, presence, humility, curiosity, and reliability—serves as an essential pillar in creating the conditions necessary for the survivor to take the leap of faith required for healing. These characteristics act as the steady hand that guides the survivor through their pain and toward resilience.

As this journey of healing unfolds, the survivor is empowered by the presence, authenticity, and compassion of their fair witness. The fair witness not only helps the survivor process their trauma but also aids in the development of new beliefs and behaviors that align with the survivor's true worth. This process goes beyond mere recovery; it is about helping the survivor live the full, authentic life they deserve.

Through the secure relationship with their fair witness, the survivor begins to see themselves as resilient and worthy, capable of forming relationships rooted in mutual respect and safety. The fair witness acts as a mirror, reflecting back the survivor's inherent strength and capacity for healing. As the survivor internalizes this belief, they are empowered to challenge their old patterns, step out of the shadows of their trauma, and move forward with hope.

This all said, **Beyond the Shiny Object** is about transformation—helping trauma survivors move beyond the distractions of surface-level behaviors and into the deep work of healing and growth. Guided by the belief and presence of their fair witness, survivors are equipped to embrace a future of resilience, strength, and hope. They learn to trust their own instincts, rebuild relationships on a foundation of authenticity, and live the full lives they deserve.

By taking the leap of faith necessary for true healing, survivors can step confidently into a future filled with new meaning, connection, and the possibility of post-traumatic growth. This journey, supported by the fair witness, leads not only to recovery but to a life lived fully and authentically beyond the trauma that once defined them.

Testimonials

"I started reading it and couldn't put it down. Rod's stories are so interesting. Each chapter makes you think about applying the lesson to your own life."
Sue Burnett, *CEO Burnett Specialists*

"*Week Minded* feels deeply personal from the first page. You can tell it was written by someone who has lived a full professional life and never lost sight of what matters most. He writes the way he leads—thoughtfully, honestly, and with real care for the people involved. What stands out about *Week Minded* is how genuine it is. Rod isn't preaching or positioning himself as an authority. He's sharing lessons the same way he would in a conversation—openly, with humility, and without ego. *Week Minded* is a reminder that strong leadership starts with kindness, listening, and doing the right thing even when it's hard. Rod's stories reinforce that you can be thoughtful and principled, practical and human, all at the same time. I'd recommend this book to anyone who values authentic leadership and believes that how you treat people really does matter."
Hang Bower, *Founder/CEO Ethos Consulting LC*

"It's a direct, no-nonsense 52-week guide for people who want results. Each week delivers one clear principle you can actually apply – to how you lead, how you work, how you make decisions, and how you run your life. It's practical thinking, uncomfortable truths, and steady pressure in the right direction. What makes this guide powerful is its discipline. One week at a time for reflection and action. It doesn't try to change you overnight; it builds consistency, judgment, and resilience over a year. The lessons compound. It's a refreshing way to approach growth and change."
Janette Marx, *CEO, Employbridge*

"Rod Branch has crafted a rare book that feels like messages from a mentor who has lived a life rich with stories, family, and friends. It shows us that our passions and 'red threads' shape us in ways we often only recognize later. This is Rod's voice at its truest: encouraging, grounded, and full of love for the reader."
Juliet Breeze, *MD, CEO, Next Level Medical*

"Rod brings an incredible amount of depth with the vast and vivid depictions of stories that bring further relevance to his journey. I so enjoyed reading the myriad of anecdotes that show an individual who has a passion for learning and knowledge woven into the fabric of the story. Rod's book is a must-read for anyone interested in the art of leadership & continuous learning. Rod has a great knack for storytelling that kept me on the edge of my seat for the entire book. I wholeheartedly endorse this wonderful depiction of a life well-lived."
Alan Brush, *Partner, Solution Spark*

"Rod Branch has crafted a masterclass in transformative insight, wrapped in a warm embrace – like curling into a warm blanket on a crisp day. The perfect blend of self-care and rest for the nervous system: soothing, grounding, and deeply human."
Sarah Kouba, *GM, Lone Star Groundwater Conservation District*

"Rod's stories and life lessons feel like sitting down with a trusted friend over a warm cup of coffee and a conversation that stays with you long after it ends. *Week-Minded* will strengthen your spirit. This isn't simply a collection of stories and wisdom — it is a guide to living with transparency, authenticity, and genuine care for others."
Liz Townsend, *Senior Partner, Allen Austin Consulting*

"People sometimes brag about 'graduating from the school of hard knocks' like it's a badge of honor to fumble through life. I'm thankful when people like Rod go out and do difficult things, learn hard lessons, gather and curate a lifetime of those lessons, and then present them on a platter for all of us to gain wisdom so we don't endure the same struggles."
Julian Pugh, *Division Operations Manager*

"I enjoy the honesty, vulnerability and relatability of your stories. I would use this as a nightly chapter read to turn my brain off from electronics and work, and read something *real* to unwind and feel the humanity of it."
Heidi Peters, *Sales Manager*